OPEN MEETINGS

and Local Governments
in North Carolina:
Some Questions and Answers

Eighth Edition 2017

Frayda S. Bluestein
David M. Lawrence

UNC
SCHOOL OF GOVERNMENT

The School of Government at the University of North Carolina at Chapel Hill works to improve the lives of North Carolinians by engaging in practical scholarship that helps public officials and citizens understand and improve state and local government. Established in 1931 as the Institute of Government, the School provides educational, advisory, and research services for state and local governments. The School of Government is also home to a nationally ranked Master of Public Administration program, the North Carolina Judicial College, and specialized centers focused on community and economic development, information technology, and environmental finance.

As the largest university-based local government training, advisory, and research organization in the United States, the School of Government offers up to 200 courses, webinars, and specialized conferences for more than 12,000 public officials each year. In addition, faculty members annually publish approximately 50 books, manuals, reports, articles, bulletins, and other print and online content related to state and local government. The School also produces the *Daily Bulletin Online* each day the General Assembly is in session, reporting on activities for members of the legislature and others who need to follow the course of legislation.

Operating support for the School of Government's programs and activities comes from many sources, including state appropriations, local government membership dues, private contributions, publication sales, course fees, and service contracts.

Visit sog.unc.edu or call 919.966.5381 for more information on the School's courses, publications, programs, and services.

Michael R. Smith, Dean
Thomas H. Thornburg, Senior Associate Dean
Frayda S. Bluestein, Associate Dean for Faculty Development
Johnny Burleson, Associate Dean for Development
Michael Vollmer, Associate Dean for Administration
Linda H. Weiner, Associate Dean for Operations
Janet Holston, Director of Strategy and Innovation

FACULTY

Whitney Afonso
Trey Allen
Gregory S. Allison
David N. Ammons
Ann M. Anderson
Maureen Berner
Mark F. Botts
Anita R. Brown-Graham
Peg Carlson
Leisha DeHart-Davis
Shea Riggsbee Denning
Sara DePasquale
James C. Drennan
Richard D. Ducker
Robert L. Farb
Norma Houston

Cheryl Daniels Howell
Jeffrey A. Hughes
Willow S. Jacobson
Robert P. Joyce
Diane M. Juffras
Dona G. Lewandowski
Adam Lovelady
James M. Markham
Christopher B. McLaughlin
Kara A. Millonzi
Jill D. Moore
Jonathan Q. Morgan
Ricardo S. Morse
C. Tyler Mulligan
Kimberly L. Nelson
David W. Owens

LaToya B. Powell
William C. Rivenbark
Dale J. Roenigk
John Rubin
Jessica Smith
Meredith Smith
Carl W. Stenberg III
John B. Stephens
Charles Szypszak
Shannon H. Tufts
Vaughn Mamlin Upshaw
Aimee N. Wall
Jeffrey B. Welty
Richard B. Whisnant

© 2017 School of Government, The University of North Carolina at Chapel Hill

Use of this publication for commercial purposes or without acknowledgment of its source is prohibited. Reproducing, distributing, or otherwise making available to a non-purchaser the entire publication, or a substantial portion of it, without express permission, is prohibited.

Printed in the United States of America

21 20 19 18 17   1 2 3 4 5

ISBN 978-1-56011-878-7

♾ This publication is printed on permanent, acid-free paper in compliance with the North Carolina General Statutes.

♻ Printed on recycled paper

Contents

Preface

Earlier editions of this book were published in 1976, 1979, 1986, 1991, 1994, 1998, 2002, and 2008. This edition incorporates legislative changes and judicial interpretations through 2016. As with the earlier editions, this book is intended for lawyers as well as members of local government governing boards, local government administrators, reporters, citizens, and others who deal on a recurring basis with the state's open meetings statute. It discusses the statute through a series of questions and short answers, with no attempt at extended argument or analysis. This edition also includes related content regarding meetings, hearings, and public comment periods. In addition, it provides a basic overview of the law, which covers many of the most commonly asked questions, and includes a quick-reference guide to closed sessions. Previous editions of this publication were written by David Lawrence, whose authoritative work in the field spans decades, and whose analysis has several times been adopted in cases decided by the North Carolina appellate courts.

Frayda S. Bluestein
David M. Lawrence Professor of Public
Law and Government

David M. Lawrence
William Rand Kenan Jr. Professor of
Public Law and Government

Chapel Hill
January 2017

An Overview of the Open Meetings Law

North Carolina's open meetings law, first enacted in 1971, provides for broad public access to meetings of public bodies. The purpose of the law "is a simple and salutary one," according to the North Carolina Supreme Court: "It is to insure that the business of the public be conducted in the view of the public so that the people may have the wherewithal to be better informed."[1] The key components of the law are as follows.

- Members of the public have a right to attend all official meetings of public bodies. The statute defines *public bodies* broadly to include all types of public boards and commissions. The definition also includes committees of those boards and commissions. Official meetings occur when a majority of the members of the public body meet to transact the business of the public body.
- Exceptions in the law allow public bodies to meet in closed session to discuss certain topics. Closed sessions are parts of open meetings, as the statute requires that they must be announced and adjourned in open session. So even if the closed session is the sole purpose for the meeting, notice of the meeting must be given, and the public has a right to attend before the closed session begins and after the closed session matter is concluded.
- An essential aspect of the law requires public notice of meetings. The law delineates four categories of

---

1. Student Bar Ass'n Bd. of Governors of School of Law, Univ. of North Carolina at Chapel Hill v. Byrd, 293 N.C. 594, 604 (1977).

meetings—regular, special, emergency, and recessed—and establishes different notice requirements for each type of meeting.

- The right of public access includes the opportunity to attend, photograph, and record meetings. There is no public right to speak at a public meeting under the open meetings law, but other provisions of law require some public bodies to provide opportunities for public comment.
- Public bodies are required to create minutes of all official meetings and general accounts of closed sessions. The legal purpose for minutes is to provide a permanent record of actions taken by the public body. It's common, though not legally required, for minutes to contain a summary of matters discussed at the meeting.
- If a public body violates the open meetings law, there is no immediate legal consequence. A person who has been denied access to an official meeting can file a lawsuit, and the law provides several remedies that a court can impose. In some cases, a public body can validate an action by convening another meeting and ratifying or repeating actions taken in the previous meeting.

Questions and Answers about the Open Meetings Law

Public Bodies

1. The open meetings law applies to "public bodies." What is a public body?

The statute defines a *public body* as any authority, board, commission, committee, council, or other body of state or local government that meets both of two conditions. First, it must have at least two members. And second, it must be authorized to exercise at least one of the following five functions: legislative, policy-making, quasi-judicial, administrative, or advisory. This definition is very broad. Special provisions also declare certain hospital corporations to be public bodies; see Question 14.

2. What about advisory boards and commissions? Are they subject to the law even if they have no authority other than to conduct studies or make recommendations?

Yes. "Advisory functions" are among those listed that make a public body subject to the law.

3. What about committees of public bodies, such as the finance committee of a city council?

They are also public bodies; the statute specifically extends to "committees."

4. What is the status of a joint board or committee established by two local governments?

It is a public body. The statute includes in the definition of public body boards and commissions of "one or more" local governments.

5. I've heard that if the mayor, a single member of a public body, or an employee such as the manager or police chief creates a committee or task force, then it's not an official public body because it wasn't created by the governing board. Is this true?

It will depend upon whether the person who created the public body had the authority to do so. A North Carolina Court of Appeals case has interpreted the statutory language defining a public body as meaning a group elected or appointed by *someone with authority to do so.*[2] A group could also become a public body if it is endorsed or supported by a person or body having the authority to create it. Evidence of such endorsement might include funding, staff support, or other resources not typically provided to private or unaffiliated groups, or actions that recognize or endorse the group and its work on behalf of the unit. In these situations, a court might hold that the open meetings law requirements apply. On the other hand, an individual public official might convene a group of advisors or citizens without invoking governmental resources and without official recognition by the unit. In this scenario, the group is not a public body and may meet with the public official in private.

6. If a group of public officials meets informally, do they constitute a public body? For example, what if all the mayors in a particular county get together for lunch to discuss common problems?

The kind of "group" involved in this example is probably not a public body. A group must have some minimal amount of structure to meet the statutory conditions. It probably should be "elected or appointed" by someone or some entity with authority to do so, rather than being self-created. In addition, such a discussion group

---

2. DTH Publ'g Corp. v. Univ. of N.C. at Chapel Hill, 128 N.C. App. 534 (1998).

is probably not exercising even one of the five required functions listed in Question 1.[3]

7. What if a single officer or employee holds some sort of formal hearing to determine, for example, whether an employee's dismissal was justified? Is that hearing a meeting of a public body?

No. A public body must include at least two people.

8. What about groups consisting of professional staff?

The statute excludes from the definition of a public body "a meeting solely among the professional staff of a public body."[4] The most likely purpose of this exception is to clarify that when groups of public employees meet to carry out the administrative work of a public body, the law does not require these meetings to be open to the public.

In some cases, however, local governments may delegate fact-finding or final decision-making authority to employee groups. A city, for example, might create a subdivision review board made up entirely of city staff, with authority to approve subdivision plats. Under a literal reading of the statute, this board would not be a public body. A court could, however, interpret the "staff only" exception to apply only when the group is engaged in staff-type work. Under this reading, a *formal* body with defined powers, constituted by law or ordinance, would be a public body regardless of its membership. Thus, the subdivision review board would be a public body, despite its membership, because it was established by city ordinance and charged with the formal power of reviewing and approving subdivisions. This ambiguity will

---

3. In *University Professionals of Illinois, Local 4100 of the Illinois Federation of Teachers v. Stukel*, 801 N.E.2d 1054 (Ill. App. Ct. 2003), the court held that a self-created "council" of presidents of the various state universities in Illinois was not a public body under that state's open meetings law; it was not created by some other entity or person.

4. N.C. GEN. STAT. (hereinafter G.S.) § 143-318.10(c).

probably be resolved only by judicial or legislative action. At least one court in another state has held that when public officials delegate their decision-making authority to staff, the staff members "stand in the shoes" of the public officials and are subject to the open meetings law.[5]

9. What if a group's membership includes some professional staff and some other persons, such as representatives of specific interest groups, members of the public, or an elected board member?

In that case the "staff only" exclusion would not apply. If such a combination group has been formally created by some person or body with authority to do so, and if the group is authorized to carry out any of the five functions listed in Question 1, the group is a public body. On the other hand, a committee comprising only staff may invite others to attend a particular meeting to consult with the group, and that intermittent presence of non-staff participants would not take the committee out of the "staff only" exception.

10. Our city appropriates money each year to a number of private nonprofit organizations. Does the fact that they receive public funds make these organizations subject to the open meetings law?

No. These funding arrangements and appropriations are essentially contracts for services, and if its only connection to the public agency is a contract, the nonprofit is not automatically subject to the open meetings law, or any other law governing public agencies. As one court in another state has noted: "[A] construction

---

5. In *Evergreen Tree Treasurers of Charlotte County, Inc. v. Charlotte County Board of County Commissioners*, 810 So. 2d 526 (Fla. Dist. Ct. App. 2002), the court held that when "public officials delegate their fact-finding duties and decision-making authority to a committee of staff members, those individuals no longer function as staff members but 'stand in the shoes of such public officials insofar as application'" of the Florida open meetings law is concerned. *Id.* at 531–32.

company that does a significant amount of road building would normally build roads pursuant to contracts with some government body. Such a company might receive up to 100% of its income from State contracts. Nevertheless, we believe that the legislature did not intend to require this type of company to open its business meetings to the public."[6] A public agency can require a nonprofit organization to comply with transparency rules as a condition of receiving funding, but the requirements do not automatically apply.

11. Aren't there some types of nonprofits that are treated as public agencies for purposes of the open meetings law?

Yes. A nonprofit organization may be subject to the law if it has other significant ties to a county, city, or other local government that extend beyond public funding. Its status will depend on the nature and breadth of those ties. One type of nonprofit organization, however—those that govern certain hospitals—is explicitly included in the statute (see Question 14).

12. Let's talk about nonprofit entities in more detail. What kinds of ties must exist for a nonprofit corporation to be subject to the law?

North Carolina courts have held that both the open meetings law and the public records law apply to nonprofit corporations when they are functionally extensions of a public agency. In the major case that dealt with this issue under the public records law, a county had created a nonprofit organization to run the county hospital.[7] The court of appeals found that the county had clear

---

6. Rockford Newspapers, Inc. v. N. Illinois Council on Alcoholism & Drug Dependence, 380 N.E.2d 1192, 1193 (1978) (holding that a contract delegating some functions and providing funding to a private entity is insufficient, by itself, to bring the private agency under the open meetings law).

7. News & Observer Publ'g Co. v. Wake Cty. Hosp. Sys., 55 N.C. App. 1 (1981).

oversight and control over the corporation, as indicated by the following factors: (1) upon its dissolution, all the corporation's assets would vest in the county; (2) all appointments to fill vacancies on the board of directors of the corporation had to be approved by the county; (3) county facilities were leased to the corporation for $1 a year; (4) the board of county commissioners was empowered to review and approve the corporation's annual budget; (5) the county was entitled to conduct a supervisory audit of the corporation; (6) the corporation was required to report its rates and charges to the county; (7) county revenue bonds financed improvements to the facilities operated by the corporation; (8) revenues collected by the corporation were county revenues for purposes of revenue bond repayment; and (9) the corporation could not change its corporate existence or amend its articles of incorporation without county consent. This pattern of supervision and control was sufficient to cause the court to hold that the corporation was an agency of the county for purposes of the public records law. In a later case, the court of appeals held that an organization created by the county and later incorporated as a nonprofit corporation remained a public body under the open meetings law.[8] Courts in other states have also extended their open meetings laws to nonprofit corporations with close ties to local or state government, but examples from other states may not necessarily apply in North Carolina.[9] That is because some states have extended public status to nonprofit organizations simply because they perform

---

8. Winfas Inc. v. Region P Human Dev. Agency, 64 N.C. App. 724 (1983).

9. Representative out-of-state cases are *News-Journal Corporation v. Memorial Hospital–West Volusia, Inc.*, 695 So. 2d 418 (Fla. Dist. Ct. App. 1997), *approved*, 729 So. 2d 373 (Fla. 1999); *Northwest Georgia Health System, Inc. v. Times-Journal, Inc.*, 461 S.E.2d 297 (Ga. Ct. App. 1995); *Andy's Ice Cream, Inc. v. City of Salisbury*, 724 A.2d 717 (Md. Ct. Spec. App. 1999); *City of Baltimore Development Corp. v. Carmel Realty Association*, 910 A.2d 406 (Md. 2006); *Souder v. Health Partners, Inc.*, 997 S.W.2d 140 (Tenn. Ct. App. 1998); and *Queen v. West Virginia University Hospital, Inc.*, 365 S.E.2d 375 (W. Va. 1987).

governmental functions or receive substantial public funding. As of yet, the North Carolina courts have extended these laws only when the nonprofit is found to be an extension of a public agency, *because the public agency exercises substantial control over the nonprofit.*

13. Is it possible for a nonprofit to avoid the transparency requirements by severing ties with a public agency?

Yes. In a North Carolina case involving a public records issue, a nonprofit organization had taken a number of steps to separate itself from its parent public agency, and the court of appeals held that it was not a government agency.[10] The case involved a housing development agency in Wilmington that was created as a nonprofit organization with significant ties to a public agency— the Wilmington Housing Authority (WHA). Factors matching those described in the Wake County Hospital case (discussed in Question 12) were eliminated over time. Changes in operations and bylaws included termination of annual review of finances and accounting by the WHA, removing the provision for assets to be transferred to the WHA upon dissolution of the nonprofit, removing the requirement for the WHA to approve bylaws changes, and reducing the WHA appointments to the board to less than a majority. The court concluded that these changes eliminated the public agency's control and, as a result, the nonprofit was no longer subject to the public records law. The same reasoning would apply under the open meetings law.

14. What nonprofit hospital corporations are subject to the open meetings law?

Those that meet any one of three qualifying definitions. First, if a hospital is owned by a county, city, hospital district, or hospital authority but is operated by a nonprofit corporation, the operating

---

10. Chatfield v. Wilmington Hous. Fin. and Dev., Inc., 166 N.C. App. 703 (2004).

corporation is a public body if a majority of its board of directors are appointed by the governing board of the county, city, hospital district, or hospital authority that owns the hospital. Second, even if the governing board does not appoint a majority of the members of the hospital corporation, the hospital directors are still a public body if a county or city has outstanding general obligation or revenue bonds issued on behalf of the hospital or if a county or city makes current appropriations (other than for the medical care of prisoners or indigents) to support the hospital. Third, if a hospital that was owned by a public entity has been sold to a nonprofit corporation under the conditions of Section 131E-8 of the North Carolina General Statutes (hereinafter G.S.), which is the only statute that permits such a sale, *the governing board* of the corporation that acquired the hospital is a public body, and so is the *governing board* of any subsidiary of that corporation or any nonprofit corporation that owns the corporation to which the hospital has been sold. If such a governing board has committees, however, the law does not seem to include the committees within the meaning of "public body."

15. What about a task force or other group that has some local government appointees, but also includes members appointed by private organizations? Would this group be considered a public body?

That depends on how large the group is, how many of its members are appointed by government, and what other ties there are between the group and one or more local governments. If the group has thirty members, for example, and only ten are appointed by local governments, and if there are no other significant ties between the group and a local government of the sort listed in the Question 12, then the group is probably not a public body. But if a majority of the members are appointed by government, and there are additional connections to government that match those described in the cases, this type of group may be subject to the law.

16. What about volunteer fire departments? Many of them are nonprofit organizations. And although the factors of public control described by the courts are not typical of their relationship with local governments, they're often completely dependent upon local government appropriations. Are they subject to the open meetings law?

Although it may seem surprising given their dependence on public funding, nothing in the statutes or case law to date requires these organizations to comply with the open meetings, public records, bidding, or other public laws. As noted in the answer to Question 10, a private entity does not become subject to the law simply by having a contract with a local government.

17. Could a local government require a volunteer fire department or other nonprofit corporation to comply with the open meetings law (or other transparency requirements) as a condition of receiving public funds?

Absolutely. A number of local governments do just that.

18. If a local government does impose such a condition on nonprofit groups that would not otherwise be subject to the open meetings law, may a citizen sue to require a recipient group to comply with the law?

Perhaps. Normally only those who are party to a contract may sue to enforce the contract, and only the granting government and the recipient agency are party to the grant contract. But sometimes courts interpret contracts as being primarily for the benefit of persons who are not party to the contract and allow these so-called third party beneficiaries to sue to enforce the contract. At least one court in another state has interpreted such a contract as evincing the parties' intent that the public have standing to enforce the contract, and therefore the open meetings law, against the agency receiving public funds.[11]

---

11. *See* State *ex rel.* Journal/Sentinel, Inc. v. Pleva, 456 N.W.2d 359 (Wis. 1990). *See also* David M. Lawrence, "Third Party Beneficiaries of

19. When a vacancy occurs on the board of county commissioners in our county, G.S. 153A-27.1 requires the remaining commissioners to fill the vacancy with the person recommended by the county executive committee of the party to which the person who held the seat belonged. Is the county executive committee a public body?

Probably not. The county executive committee is not a body created by the state or any local government.[12] A court might, nonetheless, consider it a state or county committee whenever it exercises some sort of public power, such as selecting a person to fill a vacancy on the board of county commissioners.

Official Meetings

20. The law is triggered when there is an official meeting of a public body. What's an "official meeting"?

An official meeting occurs whenever a *majority* of the members of a public body gather together *simultaneously*—in person or by some electronic means (such as a conference telephone call or an Internet or phone video conversation)—in order to

- conduct a hearing,
- participate in deliberation,
- vote, or
- otherwise transact public business.[13]

Contracts Entered into by Local Governments," *Local Government Law Bulletin* 126 (School of Government, December 2011).

12. Fuller v. Republican Cent. Comm. of Carroll Cty., 120 A.3d 751 (Md. 2015) (central political committees are not public bodies, and the members of those committees are not public officers, but, rather, party officers).

13. G.S. 143-318.10(d).

The last category is quite broad, potentially encompassing any activity that involves any matter relating to the work of the public body.

21. I thought I read elsewhere that an official meeting takes place whenever two members of the public body meet on official business.

No, that's not correct. It's easy to confuse the definition of "public body" with that of "official meeting." A *public body* is any elected or appointed group with at least *two* members. An *official meeting* takes place whenever a *majority* of the members of the public body meet on official business.[14] So the number needed to hold an official meeting will differ from public body to public body, depending on how many members each body has.

22. The answer to Question 20 states that an official meeting can take place electronically, such as through a conference telephone call. Could such a meeting also take place by email?

Yes, it's possible, depending on the specific circumstances. No North Carolina case has addressed this issue to date, but courts in other states have. Under the North Carolina statute, an official meeting requires that a majority of the body gather together *simultaneously.* Most email communications are not simultaneous. A case decided by the Virginia Supreme Court held that multiple emails among board members "did not involve sufficient simultaneity to constitute a meeting," and that "the Board

---

14. In *Gannett Pacific Corp. v. City of Asheville*, 178 N.C. App. 711 (2006), the city council and county commissioners had engaged a mediator to help settle a dispute between the two boards. Each board gathered separately at a local hotel, with appropriate notice to the public, and held a closed session to give instructions to their attorney about the mediation. Then one member from each board, along with one or more attorneys representing each board, met with the mediator. The court held that the actual mediation sessions were not official meetings of either board, because neither board had a majority present at the mediation.

[member]'s e-mails that involved some sort of back-and-forth exchange were between only two members at a time, rather than the three required."[15] It is unclear how close to contemporaneous email communications have to be for a North Carolina court to consider the exchange a simultaneous gathering within the meaning of the statute. Courts in some states, however, have recognized non-simultaneous email or other electronic communications as meetings.[16]

23. If a board member sends or receives an email that includes a majority of the board, or responds with a "reply all" to the whole board, does that constitute an official meeting?

Although North Carolina courts have not addressed this issue, cases from other states have required more than the passive sending or receipt of an email to find that a meeting has occurred.[17] The Washington Supreme Court held that "[i]f communications do not reflect the requisite collective intent to meet, no 'meeting' has occurred and the [open meetings law] does not apply."[18] Some interaction or engagement among the group would likely be required for an email exchange to be considered an official meeting. Members should therefore exercise caution when sending and receiving group emails, and should avoid participating in a series of emails by responding to all.

---

15. Hill v. Fairfax Cty. School Bd., 727 S.E.2d 75, 78–79 (Va. 2012).

16. *See* Wood v. Battle Ground Sch. Dist., 27 P.3d 1208, 1217 (Wash. App. 2001); Del Papa v. Bd. of Regents of the Univ. and Cmty. Coll. Sys. of Nevada, 956 P.2d 770 (Nev. 1998) (a meeting occurred under the Nevada open meetings law when the chair of the board of regents sent a fax to board members regarding a proposed media statement, board members responded to the chair by telephone, with the result that the faxed statement was never issued).

17. *See* Lambert v. McPherson, 98 So. 3d 30, 34 (Ala. App. 2012) (citing Wood v. Battle Ground Sch. Dist., 27 P.3d 1208, 1217 (Wash. App. 2001) ("A single e-mail sent by one board member to the other board members, without more, does not constitute a 'meeting.'").

18. Citizens All. for Prop. Rights Legal Fund v. San Juan Cty., 359 P.3d 753, 761 (Wash. 2015).

24.   What about real-time audio and visual communications over Internet-connected computers or mobile devices? A meeting using this type of technology would surely be covered by the statute.

Yes it would, assuming it involves a majority of the public body and the group is discussing public business. This would be an example of a public body simultaneously gathering together electronically. Public bodies would need to provide notice of and access to this type of meeting. Another legal issue that might arise in this situation is whether the specific type of board involved may have such a meeting at all. As discussed in the answer to Question 216, the open meetings law sets rules for electronic meetings but does not provide authority for such meetings for any particular type of public body. A public body should determine whether it has the legal authority to hold a meeting in which some or all members are participating remotely.

25.   Back to the basic definition of official meetings. Holding a hearing and taking action are both fairly clear. But what does it mean to "deliberate"?

In one court's words, "[t]o 'deliberate' is to examine, weigh and reflect upon the reasons for or against" a possible decision. "Deliberation thus connotes not only collective discussion, but the collective acquisition and exchange of facts preliminary to the ultimate decision."[19]

---

19. Sacramento Newspaper Guild v. Sacramento Cty. Bd. of Supervisors, 69 Cal. Rptr. 480, 485. (Cal. Ct. App. 1968). Other decisions that have defined "deliberate" in a similarly broad fashion are *Brookwood Area Homeowners Association, Inc. v. Municipality of Anchorage,* 702 P.2d 1317 (Alaska 1985); *Saint Cloud Newspapers, Inc. v. District 742 Community School,* 332 N.W.2d 1 (Minn. 1983); *Board of Trustees v. Mississippi Publishers Corp.,* 478 So. 2d 269 (Miss. 1985); *Ackerman v. Upper Mt. Bethel Township,* 567 A.2d 1116 (Pa. Commw. Ct. 1989); *Acker v. Texas Water Commission,* 790 S.W.2d 299 (Tex. 1990); and *McComas v. Board of Educ. of Fayette County,* 475 S.E.2d 280 (W. Va.

the matter was never considered at a board meeting. The court of appeals held that "an action by the Board to give itself a pay raise must be deliberated at a meeting open to the public. We find that such deliberations and actions are exactly the type of 'deliberations' and 'actions' that the General Assembly intended be conducted openly at a public meeting."[26]

34.　What if the manager polls the board about a matter within the manager's authority, before making a decision? Does that violate the open meetings law?

No. In this case, since the manager has the individual authority to make the decision, there is no requirement for the board to meet. The manager has no legal obligation to consult with the board as a group and is free to do so individually so long as the purpose is to get input and the matter does not ultimately involve a decision to be made by the board.[27]

35.　Don't these polling or individual procedures violate the spirit of the law?

Some might make that argument, especially when one-on-one meetings or meetings of small groups involve discussion of key policy decisions or controversial issues. On the other hand, individual public officials do have the right to meet with their

---

26. Jacksonville Daily News v. Onslow Cty. Bd. of Educ., 113 N.C. App. 127, 130 (1993); *see also* Harris v. City of Fort Smith, 197 S.W.3d 461, 467 (Ark. 2004) ("The purpose of the one-on-one meetings was to obtain a decision of the Board as a whole on the purchase of the Fort Biscuit property.").

27. *See* McCutchen v. City of Fort Smith, 425 S.W.3d 671, 679 (Ark. 2012) (distinguishing *Harris*, 197 S.W.3d 461: "In *Harris*, the one-on-one meetings between the City Administrator and the Board members ran afoul of the FOIA because the purpose of the meetings was to obtain approval of action to be taken by the Board as a whole. . . . In this case, the purpose of [the administrator's] memorandum was to provide background information on an issue that would be discussed at an upcoming study session.").

colleagues individually and in small groups, and the law requires public access only when a majority of the board is gathered together simultaneously. The legality of polling or individual and small group consultations will likely turn on the purpose and outcomes of those consultations. The only North Carolina case to hold that a non-simultaneous consultation among board members violated the law found that the process resulted in a decision that was never discussed or voted on in a public meeting.[28] On the other hand, the North Carolina Court of Appeals has upheld a process structured to exclude the public from discussions by meeting with less than a majority of the board to consider proposals for a mediated settlement of a lawsuit.[29] The court found that the board had not structured the mediation with the intent to evade the spirit and purposes of the law. Rather, "[t]he function of the mediation was to negotiate terms of the agreement," recognizing that no final action on the agreement could be taken without a majority present.[30]

36. What if a majority of board members who are up for reelection appear together at a candidate forum, or even run as a

---

28. *Jacksonville Daily News*, 113 N.C. App. at 130.

29. Gannett Pacific Corp. v. City of Asheville, 178 N.C. App. 711 (2006).

30. *Id.* at 716. *See also* Tel. Herald, Inc. v. City of Dubuque, 297 N.W.2d 529, 533 (Iowa 1980) (holding that one-on-one interviews with manager candidates did not violate the open meetings law and concluding that "such laws do not prohibit gatherings of less than a majority of the governing body where decisions are not made and official actions are not taken and . . . the right of free speech might be violated by a law forbidding any discussion by public officers between meetings"); Dewey v. Redevelopment Agency of City of Reno, 64 P.3d 1070, 1075 (Nev. 2003) ("The spirit and policy behind [the open meetings law] favors open meetings . . . . However, we have also acknowledged that the Open Meeting Law is not intended to prohibit every private discussion of a public issue. Instead, the Open Meeting Law only prohibits collective deliberations or actions where a quorum is present.").

slate? Is their appearance at the forum, or are any meetings they might have about the campaign, official meetings of the board?

Probably not. They are not meeting as board members carrying out their responsibilities as a board, but rather as candidates.[31] Board members should avoid privately discussing and developing consensus on matters currently before the board. A court might have difficulty distinguishing between a jointly held position on a campaign issue and unlawful efforts to gain consensus on a matter pending before the board.

37. What about newly elected board members who are not yet sworn in? They might constitute a majority of the new board, either by themselves or in combination with incumbents. If they get together to discuss the business of the board before they're sworn into office, would this gathering be considered an official meeting?

Probably not. Until they are sworn into office, they are still private citizens and are not yet part of a public body. For the same reason, they would not be eligible to obtain confidential information or attend closed sessions limited to board members (such as those involving personnel information or information within the attorney–client privilege) until they take the oath of office and become official members of the public body.[32]

---

31. *See* Nabhani v. Coglianese, 552 F. Supp. 657 (N.D. Ill. 1982) (meeting of board members ruled a gathering for political purposes; absent evidence of discussion of public business, exclusion of public deemed lawful).

32. *See* Kuehnapfel v. Chintall, 2014 WL 3407229 (unpublished) (N.J. 2014); Yeoman v. Commonwealth, 983 S.W.2d 459, 474 (Ky. 1998); Beck v. Shelton, 593 S.E.2d 195 (Va. 2004); Wood v. Battle Ground Sch. Dist., 27 P.3d 1208 (Wash. Ct. App. 2001).

38. When our board interviews candidates for the job of manager, do the interviews constitute deliberations?

Yes. Under the language quoted in Question 25, such interviews are part of the "collective acquisition . . . of facts" and thus deliberations.[33] In addition, the board is clearly transacting public business when it engages in such interviews. As described later, these interviews may be conducted in closed session under the personnel exception in the statute.[34]

39. What about a briefing, when the board is simply receiving information and not discussing it?

This amounts to deliberating, too. Again, the board is collectively acquiring the information on the basis of which it will act, which is part of the deliberative process.[35]

40. Are retreats official meetings under the law?

The word "retreat" has a pretty elastic meaning, and, except in regard to county commissioners, the answer depends on the purpose of the retreat. If the purpose is to provide personal skills training for individual members of the public body—such as a two-day session in facilitative leadership—no deliberation is going on, and as long as no public business is discussed, the session might not be an official meeting. The Missouri Court of Appeals held that a retreat held for that type of purpose was not a meeting under that state's open meetings law, although the Mississippi Supreme Court reached a contrary conclusion under its law.[36]

---

33. Sacramento Newspaper Guild v. Sacramento Cty. Bd. of Supervisors, 69 Cal. Rptr. 480, 485 (Cal. Ct. App. 1968); Gerstein v. Superintendent Search Screening Comm., 541 N.E.2d 984, 987 (Mass. 1989) (holding that interviews were meetings subject to the open meetings law).

34. See Question 135.

35. *See* Goodson Todman Enters., Ltd. v. City of Kingston Common Council, 550 N.Y.S.2d 157 (N.Y. App. Div. 1990).

36. Kansas City Star Co. v. Fulson, 859 S.W.2d 934 (Mo. Ct. App. 1993); Gannett River States Pub. Corp, Inc. v. City of Jackson, 866 So. 2d 462 (Miss. 2004).

But if the purpose is individual skills training as applied to, or in the context of, actual issues the board faces, or if the training is designed to discuss policy matters affecting the public body's jurisdiction, then the discussions are deliberations and the session is an official meeting. The Minnesota Supreme Court has held that even a discussion of long-range concerns is an official meeting under that state's open meetings law, and the Tennessee Court of Appeals has also held that a retreat is an official meeting.[37] (North Carolina boards of county commissioners are subject to a special rule, imposed by G.S. 153A-40, that appears to include both types of retreat within the meaning of official meeting.)

41. When a majority of the board members is seen together interacting at a dinner or social occasion, or even standing in the parking lot talking after a meeting, is that an illegal meeting?

The statute specifically permits "social gatherings" of board members, even though board business may well be mentioned in passing.[38] However, this exception cannot be used to camouflage deliberations. The purpose of the social-gatherings exception is to permit the occasional dinner, reception, or backyard barbecue. If a board meets and conducts business over breakfast or lunch, or has dinner with each final candidate for county manager, such occasions are official meetings.

42. What happens if a majority of a public body attends an external event? Does someone have to leave in order to avoid violating the law? Is the local government required to provide notice?

Not necessarily. If the event is a social occasion, there is no legal issue, as long the members avoid talking about or otherwise

---

37. Saint Cloud Newspapers, Inc. v. Dist. 742 Cmty. Sch., 332 N.W.2d 1 (Minn. 1983); Neese v. Paris Special Sch. Dist., 813 S.W.2d 432 (Tenn. Ct. App. 1990).

38. G.S. 143-318.10(d). *See* Colombo v. Buford, 935 S.W.2d 690 (Mo. Ct. App. 1996) (social event in a private home was not a meeting of the school board despite general discussion of educational philosophy).

transacting public business. But what if the event involves public business? Examples of such settings include conferences or training sessions, political events, meetings with state or federal legislators, and meetings of other public bodies. A key question in this situation is whether the board is "meeting," "assembled," or "gathered" within the meaning of the open meetings law. To date, North Carolina's appellate courts have yet to address the meaning of these terms, but cases from other states have concluded that a meeting or gathering necessarily requires some evidence of a *collective intention to come together as a group.* For example, in holding that the passive receipt of emails does not constitute a meeting, the Washington Supreme Court held that "a 'meeting' of a governing body occurs when a majority of its members gathers *with the collective intent of transacting the governing body's business . . .* "[39] In another case, four members of a school board (a majority) attended an event for local elected officials. They received individual invitations to the event and did not coordinate their attendance. The court held that although a majority attended the event, the evidence did not show that the members had gathered or came together as a group to transact public business. As such, their simultaneous presence at the event did not constitute a "meeting," as defined by the relevant statute.[40]

The following factors should be considered when determining when the presence of a majority of a public body at external events triggers the notice requirements.

- *What is the purpose and nature of the event?* If it is a social event or activity that does not involve matters within the scope or jurisdiction of the public body, then attendance will not constitute an official meeting so long as the members attending refrain from gathering as a group to discuss public business.

---

39. Citizens All. for Prop. Rights Legal Fund v. San Juan Cty., 359 P.3d 753, 761 (Wash. 2015) (*emphasis added*).
40. Slagle v. Ross, 125 So. 3d 117 (Ala. 2012).

- *Was attendance planned or prearranged by the public body?* If there was no coordination and members individually made the decision to attend, their simultaneous presence does not, by itself, constitute an official meeting under the statute.
- *Did the members transact business at the event?* Even if the event is a social one, and even if the members independently made the decision to attend, they can still run afoul of the law if a majority of them gather together at the event and transact public business.

As noted earlier, a public body may transact business through deliberation, which can occur even when a board gathers together to simply observe and obtain information. A Wisconsin case provides an example of a situation in which a board's collective decision regularly to attend meetings of another board triggered the open meetings law. The court ruled that notice was required when a majority of the village board regularly attended meetings of the village plan commission, including several meetings regarding a proposed housing project. They listened to the discussion, but did not participate or engage in discussion among themselves. Nonetheless, the court noted that the commission was considering a matter over which the village board would exercise final control. The board was obtaining information about the project—a type of deliberation—and the public should have had notice of the existence of this information and its relevance to the board's decision-making process.[41] A key finding in this case was that attendance at these meetings was not a chance event. Instead it was a regular practice of the board members to attend these meetings. The North Carolina statute appears to require some level of intent to gather as a group. So if a majority of board members sep-

---

41. State *ex rel.* Badke v. Village Bd. of Village of Greendale, 494 N.W.2d 408, 415 (Wis. 1993).

arately and independently show up at a meeting, notice probably *would not* be required under the North Carolina statute, so long as they don't gather together or interact as a group while at the meeting, and provided that attendance by a majority of members does not become a regular practice.

43. What if a majority of the board plans to attend a community meeting conducted by the planning department, for example, or the police chief? Is this an official meeting?

To answer this question, apply the three factors from the preceding question. First, what is the purpose and nature of the event? In this case, it clearly involves matters within the jurisdiction of the public body and is not a social event. Second, is attendance planned or pre-arranged? If the individual members independently decide to attend, their attendance probably does not constitute an official meeting. Third, will the members transact business? If the members don't gather together or discuss official business during the meeting, a court would likely find that an official meeting did not occur.

44. What about a visit by a majority of members of a public body to inspect another county's 911 system, a piece of heavy equipment, or a landfill site? Is that kind of inspection trip an official meeting?

Probably, even though there are obvious difficulties in providing for public access on such a visit. If, as Question 25 suggests, "deliberations" include the collective acquisition of information that will later be used to make a decision, then an inspection trip meets the definition of an official meeting. In addition, the group is clearly transacting public business. Courts in other states have held a comparable visit to be a meeting under those states' open meetings laws.[42]

This situation can be particularly challenging when the site visit occurs on private property. In some cases the owner may be unwilling to open the property to the public at large or have concerns about liability for citizens who might want to attend. Under these circumstances it may be both practical and justifiable for the public body to conduct the site visit in groups to avoid violating the statute.

45. Our board members commonly attend ceremonial activities, such as ribbon cuttings, swearing-in ceremonies, retirement, or other employee recognition events. Are these official meetings?

Probably not. Some of these events may be considered social events, but even so, the members are clearly there in an official capacity. Nonetheless, these occasions may not actually involve the transaction of public business in the sense contemplated by the statute. A Nebraska Supreme Court case held that the passive attendance at a ceremonial event did not violate that state's open meetings act. The court held that the event did not involve the type of activity targeted by the statute: "[T]he secret formation of policy prohibited by the Open Meetings Act refers to the formation of such policy as a group. This implies some communication between a meaningful number of its members, from which the public has been excluded . . . there is likewise no meeting of a

---

42. *See* Gold Country Estates Preservation Group, Inc. v. Fairbanks North Star Borough, 270 P.3d 787, 796 (Alaska 2012) ("[I]nformation-gathering and discussion at the site visit constituted collective consideration of 'a matter upon which the governmental body [was] empowered to act' and a key step in the 'deliberative and decision-making process . . .'"); State *ex rel.* Murray v. Palmgren, 646 P.2d 1091 (Kan. 1982) (involving a visit by a hospital board of trustees to another city to interview an applicant for the position of hospital administrator); Alderman v. Cty. of Antelope, 653 N.W.2d 1 (Neb. Ct. App. 2002) (the court and all parties agreed that a visit by a majority of the county board of supervisors to a dairy seeking a conditional use permit was an official meeting under the Nebraska open meetings law).

public body when, although there is a quorum present, there is no interaction as to the policy in question."[43]

46. The answers to Questions 10 through 13 noted that some entities organized as private nonprofit corporations are nevertheless treated as public agencies under the open meetings law. G.S. 55A-8-21 permits the board of directors of a North Carolina nonprofit corporation to take action without a meeting, simply through the written consent of each board member. How does the open meetings law impact that statutory authority?

Most likely the open meetings law does not change that statutory authority. A governmental entity, such as an elected governing board, may only act while convened in a meeting. This is one reason why an attempt by such a board to act outside a meeting violates the open meetings law; it is a ploy to avoid open-meetings responsibilities. But since a nonprofit corporation's board of directors is permitted by statute to act without being in a meeting, acting pursuant to that statutory authority is not simply a ploy to avoid the open meetings law.

Notice Requirements

General Questions

47.   What are the notice requirements for official meetings?

The law delineates four categories of meetings—regular, special, emergency, and recessed—and establishes different notice requirements for each type. These requirements are discussed in more detail below. Additional notice requirements apply to meetings of local governing boards and there are separate notice requirements for some kinds of public hearings. These are discussed in

---

43. *See* Schauer v. Grooms, 786 N.W.2d 909, 927 (Neb. 2010).

the Related Public Meeting Topics section of this publication in Questions 230–242.

48. What if two boards are going to meet together for a joint discussion? Which body should give the required notice?

Both are responsible for giving notice of the meeting.

49. Is notice required when a majority of the members are attending an external event?

As discussed in Question 42, the mere presence of a majority of a public body does not necessarily constitute an official meeting. Here are some guidelines for determining when notice is required for external events:

- There is **no need to provide notice** of the fact that a majority of a public body will or may attend an event that is purely social and does not involve the transaction of public business. *If a group comprising a majority of the members of the public body engages in conversation or deliberation about public business at such an event, it will be violating the law.*
- There is **no need to provide notice** of the fact that a majority of a public body will or may be present at an event—even one that is not purely social—if the attendance of the members is not preplanned by the public body, and if a majority of members will not interact or engage in the transaction of public business at the event.
- If a public body (or a majority of a public body) plans as a group to attend an event that relates to public business, even if the purpose is only to observe, **notice should be provided**. Although no North Carolina case has addressed this issue to date, a reasonable interpretation of the statute's language suggests that when a majority of a public body intentionally gathers together to attend a meeting involving public business, an official meeting occurs and notice should be provided.

Regular Meetings

50. What notice is required for regular meetings?

If a public body holds regular meetings, at a fixed time and place (and not all bodies do), the law requires two forms of notice. First, the schedule of those regular meetings must be filed in a central location. For a city council and each other public body that is part of a city government, the central filing location is the office of the city clerk. For a board of county commissioners and each other public body that is part of a county government, the central filing location is the office of the clerk to the board of commissioners. State public bodies file their schedules with the secretary of state. The schedule of any other public body that is not part of a city or county government, nor of state government, is to be filed with its own clerk or secretary. Second, if the public body has a website, it must post the schedule of regular meetings on that site.

51. Is a school administrative unit part of city or county government for filing purposes?

No. The regular meeting schedule of a school board should be filed in the superintendent's office.

52. What about a board that doesn't hold regular meetings at all?

If a board does not have a schedule of regular meetings, then all of its meetings are special meetings.

53. Is this filing the only requirement for regular meetings? Isn't it necessary to send a copy of the agenda for regular meetings to the press or post the agenda on the website?

As a matter of courtesy, many local governments do post agendas and perhaps email copies to the local news media, but no law requires them to do so. In fact, there is no requirement to have an agenda at all. The only requirements are the filing and website posting described in Question 50.

54. How often must this schedule of regular meetings be filed?

The notice is permanent and need be filed only once, unless the schedule changes. Many boards review and revise the schedule at least annually to reflect holidays and other variations that might occur.

55. What is the procedure for changing the date of a regular meeting?

A permanent change in the regular meeting schedule is made by filing a new schedule. This must be done at least seven calendar days before the first meeting that occurs under the new schedule. If only a single meeting is to be changed, or the meeting needs to be rescheduled quickly, an alternative approach is to cancel the regular meeting and reschedule it as a special meeting, giving the appropriate special meeting notice described below in Questions 58 through 70. This alternative approach, however, may limit the scope of the meeting. Boards have broad flexibility to take up any matter they choose in a regular meeting. As noted in Question 60, the notice requirement for a special meeting must include a statement of the purpose of the meeting, and thus the board may be limited to matters within the scope of the purpose described in the notice.[44] The special meeting notice could include all of the matters listed on the agenda for the cancelled regular meeting, but the board would likely not have the flexibility to add to or modify the items listed.

56. Does the open meetings law require the public body to approve a change in the regular meeting schedule?

The open meetings law does not address this. Other state laws, however, require city and county governing boards to fix the time and place for their regular meetings.[45] These provisions suggest that the board must approve a change in the schedule. Governing

---

44. See Question 67.
45. G.S. 160A-71(a) (cities); G.S. 153A-40(a) (counties).

boards of local school units are authorized to hold regular meetings, but the statute does not specifically require them to set the schedule.[46] In this case a change could be approved by staff, if the board has delegated that authority.

57. Does the law require a public body to provide notice that a meeting will be cancelled?

Nothing in the law requires such notice. If a meeting is rescheduled, the notice of the rescheduled meeting will typically provide notice of the cancellation as well. Some units also provide additional notice as a courtesy, for example by posting the information on the website and on a bulletin board or meeting room door and sending the information to individuals and groups involved in matters that were on the agenda for the cancelled meeting.

Special Meetings

58. What about special meetings, then? First of all, what is a "special meeting"?

Basically, a special meeting is any meeting—other than an emergency meeting or a recessed meeting, which we'll talk about later—that occurs at a time or place other than the time and place set out on a public body's filed schedule of regular meetings. Thus, if a public body meets at a time different from its regular meeting time or at a place different from its regular meeting place, it is holding a special meeting for notice purposes.

59. Wait a minute. What if an unexpectedly large crowd arrives for a regularly scheduled meeting and the public body decides to move to a larger room than it regularly meets in? Does the meeting become a special meeting just because the larger room is not the regular meeting place?

No. If the meeting begins at the regular meeting room, the public body may then *recess* and move to the larger room. That would

---

46. G.S. 115C-41(b).

be a recessed session and, as the answer to Question 75 notes, minimal notice is necessary. (It would be courteous to leave a notice at the regular room, so that latecomers will know where the meeting has gone.) And, as noted in the answer to Question 196, there is no absolute requirement to accommodate all members of the public who wish to attend.

60. What public notice is required for a special meeting?

The law requires three methods of notice for special meetings. Under the first two methods, notice must be given at least 48 hours before the meeting and must state the time, place, and purpose of the meeting. Normally, listing the building in which a meeting will be held is adequate notice of place, but for larger buildings it is wise to list the meeting room as well.

The first method of notice is by posting. If the public body has a principal bulletin board, the notice must be posted there. If it has no bulletin board, the notice must be posted at the door of the body's usual meeting room. The second method of notice requires mailing, emailing, or delivering the notice to each person who has submitted a written request for notice to the clerk or secretary of the public body or to some other person designated by the public body to receive these requests. The list of entities who have made this request is often referred to as the "sunshine" list. The third method is to post the notice on the public body's website, if that site is maintained by employees of the public body. The statute states that website notice must be posted before the meeting is held but does not specifically require a minimum of 48 hours of notice. Nevertheless, a public body should post the notice on its website at the same time it gives the other forms of notice.

61. If someone requests notice of city council meetings, does that mean he or she must be mailed notice of meetings of all the public bodies in city government?

No. The city must provide written notice only of the meetings of the public body or bodies listed in the request. Of course, if someone requests notice of the special meetings of all the public bodies in city government, then the city must provide notice of the special meetings of all those public bodies.

62. Aren't we supposed to advertise the special meeting in the local newspaper as well as posting notice?

No. The open meetings law never requires that meetings be advertised, although other statutes require advertisement for certain kinds of meetings, or meeting-related actions, such as public hearings. (See the Related Public Meetings Topics section of this publication.)

63. What if the 48 hours include a weekend?

If some or all of the 48 hours of posted notice occur over a weekend, or other period when the building will not be open to the public, the body must post the notice at some place that is in fact accessible to the public, either on the building door or at some other outside location.

64. What is the procedure for cancelling and rescheduling a special meeting?

The statute does not specify a procedure for cancelling a special meeting. As a courtesy, the local government can provide individual notice to those who have requested to receive notice. There is no legal requirement to do this, though. If the meeting is rescheduled for another day or time, a new 48 hours' notice is required.

65. Can the local government charge persons who request to receive notice the cost of giving notice?

The answer depends on who is requesting the notice and how it is provided. There is no authority to charge a newspaper, radio or television station, or wire service that requests notice. The law prohibits charging any requester for the cost of the notice by email. But if an individual has requested notice, and it is not provided by email, the law requires the public agency to charge that person $10 per year.[47]

66. Can these persons be required to renew their requests periodically?

Yes. The public body may require that news media renew notice requests at least annually, and other persons may be required to renew as often as every three months.[48]

67. The answer to Question 60 says that the notice of special meetings must state the purpose of the meeting. Once a public body is meeting, may it talk about subjects other than those included in the stated purpose of the meeting?

That's not clear. The law simply does not say one way or the other. Other North Carolina statutes that require notices of special meetings to include an agenda explicitly forbid transacting items of business not on that agenda unless all members are present or any members not present have signed a written waiver of notice.[49] Perhaps the silence of the open meetings law indicates that the statement of purpose, at least if made in good faith, does not limit discussion of or action on other topics. A public body should be careful about going beyond the notice, however. Appellate courts in some other states (although not all) have found violations of

---

47. G.S. 143-318.12(b)(2).
48. *Id.*
49. *See* G.S. 153A-40 (counties); G.S. 160A-71 (cities).

their open meetings laws when items not in the notice were discussed and acted upon.[50]

A public body should be especially careful about adding topics to the agenda of a special meeting when the original purpose of the meeting, as stated in the notice, is to hold a closed session. Such notice may well discourage many citizens from attending the meeting; therefore, the body probably should not extend the meeting's purposes to include matters that must be discussed in an open session. A court might well find such a sequence of events misleading to the public.

68. What about the opposite? Is there any obligation to consider all the matters included in the notice of a special meeting?

No. A board can always decide not to consider a matter that appears on its agenda.[51]

69. How detailed does the statement of purpose need to be? If, for example, the notice states that the public body will "consider" a matter, may the public body act on that matter?

We don't know for sure. No North Carolina appellate cases have addressed this issue, and the cases from other states reach opposing results. If there is any chance a public body might act on a matter at a special meeting, it is good practice to give warning of that possibility in the notice of the meeting.[52]

---

50. *Compare* River Road Neighborhood Ass'n v. S. Texas Sports, 720 S.W.2d 551 (Tex. App. 1986) (taking action to authorize execution of a lease not permitted under notice stating that the board would "discuss" a proposed lease) *with* Law and Info. Servs., Inc. v. City of Riviera Beach, 670 So. 2d 1014 (Fla. Dist. Ct. App. 1996) (holding that unless the statute specifically forbade changing the agenda set out in the notice [which North Carolina's does not], the board controlled its own agenda and could change it at will).

51. *See* Schmidt v. Washoe Cty., 159 P.3d 1099 (Nev. 2007).

52. *See, e.g,* Tanner v. Town Council of Town of East Greenwich, 880 A.2d 784 (R.I. 2005) (notice of meeting to interview applicants

70. What about meetings to consider the annual budget? Doesn't the Budget and Fiscal Control Act provide that notice is not required for special meetings for that purpose?

That's incorrect. G.S. 159-17 excuses a public body from some of the special-meeting notice requirements for members of the public body if the purpose of the meeting is to work on the annual budget. But the statute specifically directs that the notice required to be given to the public under the open meetings law must still be given for such sessions.

---

for board appointments insufficient to allow voting on appointments); Cty. of Monmouth v. Snyder-Westerhind Corp., 383 A.2d 740 (N.J. App. Div. 1978) (holding that a notice that the board would meet with a named attorney was insufficient to allow the board to settle a lawsuit with the party the attorney represented). *But cf.* Town of Marble v. Darien, 181 P.3d 1148, 1149 (Colo. 2008) ("[A]n ordinary member of the community would understand that the agenda item listed on the notice—Mill Site Committee Update—would include consideration of, and possible formal action on, the Mill Site Park proposal."); City of San Angelo v. Texas Natural Res. Conserv. Comm'n, 92 S.W.3d 624 (Tex. App. 2002), Odessa Texas Sheriff's Posse, Inc. v. Ector Cty., 215 S.W.3d 458 (Tex. App. 2006) (holding that "consideration" of a matter necessarily includes the possibility of acting upon it); Shirley v. Beauregard Parish Sch. Bd., 615 So. 2d 17 (La. Ct. App. 1993) (holding that a notice that said the board was to "hear recommendations" about a matter was sufficient to allow the board to act on those recommendations).

Emergency Meetings

71. Let's talk about "emergency meetings." How are they defined?

The definition has two elements. First, the meeting must concern "generally unexpected circumstances."[53] Second, those circumstances must require "immediate consideration" by the public body.[54]

72. What does it mean to say that a matter demands the "immediate consideration" of the public body?

As a practical matter, if the public body must meet on a matter before 48 hours have passed, so that the normal special-meeting notice is impossible, the matter can be considered to demand immediate consideration and the notice procedures for emergency meetings may be used. The matter in question should really be one that cannot wait 48 hours; otherwise the public body could be violating the law.[55]

73. What does it mean to say that a meeting concerns "generally unexpected circumstances"?

No North Carolina court has interpreted this language in the context of the open meetings law, but a case involving an "emergency" exception to the bidding statutes may provide useful insight into

---

53. *See River Road Neighborhood Ass'n*, 720 S.W.2d at 551 (invalidating a board's judgment that there was an emergency on the ground that the board should have anticipated the need for the meeting and therefore should have called the meeting earlier than it did, with enough time for longer notice).

54. G.S. 143-318.12(f).

55. *See* Town of Lebanon v. Wayland, 467 A.2d 1267 (Conn. Super. Ct. 1983) (holding that the public body could have delayed considering the matter at issue long enough to permit normal notice procedures to be followed; because notice was therefore inadequate, the actions taken as a result of the emergency meeting were invalidated); Steenblock v. Elkhorn Township Bd., 515 N.W.2d 128 (Neb. 1994).

its meaning. *Raynor v. Commissioners for Town of Louisburg*[56] involved a challenge to the town's purchase of diesel engines without bidding. The court rejected the town's reliance on the emergency exception in the public bidding law, finding that the fact that the engines were old and in need of replacement was foreseeable and not sufficient to justify the failure to comply with the bidding laws. The court said that "the emergency which would relieve the town council of the duty of advertising for competitive bids must be present, *immediate, and existing, and not a condition which may or may not arise . . . .*" The court further noted, "It is not to be supposed that [the legislature] intended to make it possible for municipal officers to avoid advertising for bids for public work by merely *delaying to take action to meet conditions which they can foresee* until danger to public health and safety has become so great that the slight further delay caused by advertising will entail public calamity" (emphases added).[57] A court would likely look to this standard in a case under the open meetings law. So even if a matter requires immediate consideration, it should also have been unforeseeable.

74. What notice is necessary for an emergency meeting?

All that is required is notification to any local news medium that has requested notice. Persons other than the media are not entitled to notice of emergency meetings. The manner of notice is either by telephone, by email, or in the same way the board members are notified. There is no minimum time period for this notice. The meeting may be held as quickly as the public body's members can gather.[58] (As noted in Question 233, city councils are subject to an additional statute that requires 6 hours' notice to members, even in emergencies.)

---

56. 220 N.C. 348, 353 (1941).
57. *Id.* at 354.
58. G.S. 143-318.12(b)(3).

Recessed Meetings

75. The final kind of meeting, I believe, is a "recessed meeting"?

That's right. Such a meeting takes place when a public body recesses a meeting to be resumed later. If proper notice was given of the original meeting and if the time and place of the recessed session is set in the open at the original meeting, only one further form of notice is required. If the public body has a website maintained by its employees, it must post the time and place of the recessed portion of the meeting on that site at some time before the recessed meeting occurs.[59]

76. If the public body is meeting in closed session, could it, while still in the closed session, recess the closed session to a specific time, thereby avoiding the need for further public notice of the recessed session?

Such an action is not permissible. There is no authority to take this action in closed session. In addition, the statute requires notice of the recessed meeting time and place to be announced in open session.

77. We've been talking about notice requirements under the open meetings law. Are there any other types of notice required for local government meetings?

Yes. G.S. Chapter 160A (for cities) and Chapter 153A (for counties) establish meeting requirements that are separate from the open meetings law. (There are no such provisions in Chapter 115C for local school boards.) These statutes require regular meetings, specify how and when other meetings may be called, and describe the notice that must be given to board members. In addition, some meetings may involve a public hearing, a rezoning, or other matters for which there are separate notice requirements. Both the open meetings law notice and any other specific notice must be

---

59. G.S. 143-318.12(b)(1) and (f).

provided in order for the meeting and any actions taken therein to be valid.

For more information on these provisions, see the section on Related Public Meeting Topics in this publication.

Exceptions and Closed Sessions

78. Are there exceptions to the basic requirement that all meetings be open?

Yes. The exceptions fall into two categories. First are exceptions in the General Statutes that remove several specific kinds of public bodies from the law altogether; these groups need never meet in public nor give public notice of their meetings. Only one of the groups in this category typically involves local governments. It is described in Question 176.

Second, the open meetings law lists certain subjects that may be discussed in a closed session—that is, a session from which the public is excluded.

79. What are the closed session exceptions?

There are twelve subject-matter exceptions, set out in ten sub-sections of the statute.[60] Here is a summary list of the authorized subjects.

- Confidential information
- Honorary degrees, scholarships, prizes, and awards
- Consultations with an attorney
- Business location or expansion
- Military installation closure or alignment
- Real property acquisition
- Employment contracts
- Personnel matters

---

60. G.S. 143-318.11(a)(1)–(10).

- Criminal investigations
- School violence response plans
- Anti-terrorism plans
- Viewing of body-worn, dashboard, and other law enforcement recordings

General Rules for Closed Sessions

See the Quick-Reference Guide to Closed Sessions (Appendix 1).

80. Before we consider each subject, I have several questions about closed sessions in general. First, are there special procedures for going into closed session?

Yes. The statute provides that a closed session may be held only on a motion adopted in open session by a majority of those present and voting. The motion must state the purpose set out in the statute that permits the closed session, such as "to consider matters relating to the location or expansion of industries or other businesses." In addition, two of the purposes require a more detailed motion. First, if the purpose of the closed session is to discuss a matter that is confidential by law, the motion must name or cite the law that makes the matter confidential. For example, if a county board of health meets to consider the quarantine of particular individuals who have a communicable disease, the motion to go into closed session would have to cite G.S. 130A-143, the statute that makes information about individuals with communicable diseases confidential. Second, if the purpose is to talk with an attorney about existing litigation, the motion must identify the parties to the lawsuit.

81. But what if the litigation has not yet been brought? For example, assume the public body is meeting to decide whether it has a strong enough case to bring a lawsuit itself. Must the motion list the possible parties if the suit were to be brought?

No. The requirement of more detailed notice applies only to "existing lawsuits."

82. Does the motion calling for a closed session have to cite the specific statute number and subsection in the open meetings law that permit the closed session?

No. There's no such requirement in the statute. The motion is sufficient as long as it clearly identifies or describes a permissible basis for the closed session.

83. Does the motion have to include anything more than the permissible basis? For example, if the board is going into closed session to discuss an employee or public officer, must the motion indicate the name of the employee or officer?

No. The statute does not require it, and in many cases that information would be confidential.

84. If the public body goes into closed session to discuss one matter, may it consider other matters eligible for closed-session discussion at the same time?

No. The law gives the public the right to know what general subjects are being talked about in closed sessions. Therefore, the public body must restrict its discussion to the matter or matters set out in the motion that authorized the closed session. If it wants to talk about another matter, it should return to open session and amend the original motion, or adopt a new one, stating the additional purpose. The original motion could also include both bases for the closed session, in which case the board could move from one matter to the next without going back into open session.

85. If our board intends to hold a special meeting on a matter for which a closed session is permitted, so that the entire meeting will be closed, must we give notice of the special meeting?

Yes. Notice must be given of all official meetings, and meetings devoted to closed sessions are still official meetings. Indeed, it is not legally possible for the entire meeting to be closed, since the motion to go into closed session must be made in open session.

In addition, the board must adjourn the meeting in open session since there is no authority to take this action in closed session.

86. May we hold a closed session at a retreat or a workshop meeting?

Sure. The board may hold a closed session at any official meeting.

87. Who may attend a closed session?

Only the members of the public body itself have a right to attend. The body may allow others to attend, if their presence will be useful to the discussion. The public body has broad discretion to determine which employees and staff members may attend. But without some logical basis for the distinction, it may not allow some members of the public to attend and not others.[61] A public body must be particularly careful in deciding whom to include in a closed session that involves confidential information, as attendance must be limited to those who have legal access to that information. Similarly, closed sessions held to preserve the attorney–client privilege must be limited to those who are within the privilege, as detailed in Question 105.

88. If a board is holding a properly closed meeting and a person not entitled to be present refuses to leave, what remedies does the board have?

If a person refuses to leave after being instructed to do so, that person's conduct constitutes criminal trespass, and the offender may be prosecuted under G.S. 14-159.13. In addition, if the person is disruptive and refuses to leave after being directed to do so by the presiding officer, the open meetings law itself states that the offender has committed a Class 2 misdemeanor.[62]

---

61. *See* Georgetown Commc'ns, Inc. v. Williams, 348 S.E.2d 396 (S.C. Ct. App. 1986); Smith v. Sheriff, 982 S.W.2d 775 (Mo. Ct. App. 1998); United Indep. Sch. Dist. v. Gonzalez, 911 S.W.2d 118 (Tex. App. 1995).
62. G.S. 143-318.17.

89. May two boards hold a combined closed session?

The answer depends on the purpose of the closed session. If two boards are jointly purchasing a tract of land, they could hold a joint closed session to determine their joint bargaining position in the negotiations. The same would be true if two boards were negotiating a coordinated incentives package with a single company. But if the two boards were in litigation between themselves, they could not meet jointly with the attorneys for each side to discuss settlement of the lawsuit. The authority to meet in closed session to discuss litigation is intended to preserve the attorney–client privilege. Under that exception, only those within the scope of the privilege may be present.

90. Our board has two ex-officio members. Are they entitled to attend closed sessions?

Absolutely. To be an ex-officio member means only that membership on the public body arises from some other position held by that person. He or she is a full-fledged member of the public body.

91. If only members have a right to attend, does that mean the board can exclude its chief administrator from a closed session, as when a school board does not allow the superintendent to attend?

Exactly. Again, although boards will generally invite their chief administrators to closed sessions, only members of the board itself are entitled to attend.

92. But the statutes setting out the duties of city and county managers state that the manager "shall attend" all governing board meetings.

That's right. But that language still does not entitle the manager to be present during every part of the governing board's meeting. The open meetings law specifies that the public body itself may hold the closed session.

93.   Must the clerk to the city or county governing board attend all closed sessions?

No. It is up to the board to determine whether the clerk needs to be present.

94.   Well, if only board members are there, who takes minutes or prepares the general account of the closed session?

If no staff members attend a closed session, the board must identify one of its members to prepare minutes and the general account of the closed session (see Question 178).

95.   Can action be taken in a closed session, or is the session restricted to discussion only?

There is no general prohibition on taking action in closed session. Indeed, some of the exceptions explicitly permit action to be taken in closed session, while others clearly require action to be taken in open session. For example, the provision that allows closed sessions to preserve the attorney–client privilege specifically authorizes the board to instruct the attorney in closed session regarding the handling of litigation. The personnel exception requires final action to hire or fire employees to be taken in open session but appears to permit or even require other employment actions in closed sessions. An examination of each authorization to hold a closed session is necessary to determine whether action may be taken with regard to that subject in the closed session.

96.   If action cannot be taken in closed session, may a board reach a tentative consensus in such a session and then take formal action in open session?

Yes. The North Carolina Supreme Court has construed the law to permit such a procedure.[63]

---

63. *See* Maready v. City of Winston-Salem, 342 N.C. 708, 732 (1996).

97.   Well, even if the law permits an action to be taken in closed session, wouldn't it still be necessary to confirm or announce that action in open session?

No. In those instances in which the law permits action to be taken in closed session, the purpose is to permit the substance of that action (and in some cases the fact of that action) to remain secret.

Confidential Records (G.S. 143-318(a)(1))

98.   What does the exception for confidential records permit?

This exception permits a closed session to consider information that is privileged or confidential under state or federal law or that is not a public record under state law.[64]

99.   What sorts of information might qualify for this exception?

There are many kinds of records that are confidential under state law or that are by statute excepted from the public records law. Some of these are covered by other exceptions to the open meetings law, such as those for discussions of personnel or of the location of new industries. The most important of the others are the following.

- *Medical records.* Medical and personal financial records about specific patients of health care facilities, such as public hospitals and public health departments (G.S. 131E-97).
- *Medical staff records.* Credentialing and peer review information about persons with practice privileges at public hospitals (G.S. 131E-97.2).
- *Health care contracts.* Competitive health care information in health care services contracts between hospitals and third party payors (G.S. 131E-99).

---

64. *See* DTH Publ'g Corp. v. Univ. of N.C. at Chapel Hill, 128 N.C. App. 534 (1998) (citing a substantial federal policy of confidentiality of student records, including university student records).

- *Hospital competition.* Information about competitive health care activities of public hospitals (G.S. 131E-97.3).
- *Mental health records.* Medical records about specific patients of area authorities (G.S. 122C-52).
- *Student records.* Official records of school students (G.S. 115C-402).
- *Public assistance records.* Information about persons receiving public assistance (G.S. 108A-80).
- *Criminal investigation records.* Information gathered as part of a criminal investigation (G.S. 132-1.4).
- *Local tax records.* Any information associated with the administration of a locally levied tax that reveals a taxpayer's income or gross receipts, such as a local privilege license tax measured by gross receipts or an occupancy tax (G.S. 153A-148.1; G.S. 160A-208.1).
- *Public security plans and building plans.* Information containing specific details of public security plans and arrangements or the detailed plans and drawings of public buildings and infrastructure facilities (G.S. 132-1.6).
- *Certain electric power contract discussions.* Discussions about contracts to which a joint power agency may be party, concerning electric power operations (G.S. 159B-38).

100. Might a board ever take action in closed session under this exception?

Certainly. In some cases it must do so. For example, a school board might in closed session uphold the suspension of a student. If taking an action in open session would result in public release of information that is confidential by law, such as student records, the action must, in fact, be taken in closed session.

The Attorney–Client Privilege (G.S. 143-318(a)(3))

101. What does the exception to preserve the attorney–client privilege encompass?

The attorney–client exception permits a public body to "consult with an attorney employed or retained by the public body in order to preserve the attorney–client privilege between the attorney and the public body."[65]

102. So it only covers instances in which the public body wants to say something to the attorney?

No. The attorney–client privilege protects confidential communications from the attorney to the client, as well as from the client to the attorney.

103. Does the attorney have to be present at such a closed session?

The board cannot have a closed session under this subdivision unless the session includes an attorney employed or retained by the public body. The attorney does not necessarily have to be physically present; he or she may participate remotely by telephone or other synchronous electronic means. In addition, although a client may have privileged communications with an agent of an attorney, such as the attorney's paralegal, the open meetings law itself requires that the closed session be held "to consult with an *attorney*" (emphasis added).

104. Does the attorney have to be an employee or under contract? What about a consultation with a person who is volunteering his or her services, is being considered for hire or

---

65. The topic of closed sessions held to protect the attorney–client privilege is discussed at length in David M. Lawrence, "Closed Sessions under the Attorney–Client Privilege," *Local Government Law Bulletin* 102 (School of Government, April 2002).

retention, or is giving advice before having been hired or retained by the public body?

The statute specifically applies only to attorneys retained or employed by the body, so the relationship may need to be formalized unless the attorney is considered to be an agent of the board's attorney.[66]

105. Who else may be present at a closed session under the attorney–client exception?

Although the governing board is thought of as the client of a public attorney, the client is actually the governmental entity of which the governing board is a part. Various other boards and individuals within the unit are within the scope of the attorney–client privilege and may participate in closed sessions under this exception if their presence is deemed necessary or appropriate to the matter at hand. For example, a closed session involving the city council and the city attorney might also legitimately include the city manager, the city clerk, and one or more relevant department heads.

Caution should be exercised, however, in allowing someone who is not an employee or official of the entity to attend a closed session held to protect the attorney–client privilege. The presence of an outsider—even someone such as a consultant to the governmental entity or a citizen involved in the matter under discussion—might destroy the attorney–client privilege at the meeting and thus invalidate the closed session.[67] Simply having the attorney present does not justify the closed session.

---

66. *See id.* at 5.

67. In *Brown v. American Partners Federal Credit Union*, 183 N.C. App. 529 (2007), the court of appeals discusses the various tests for deciding which organizational officials or employees might be within the organization's attorney–client privilege. The discussion reinforces the suggestion in the text that a public body should be cautious about allowing outsiders into a closed session with the public body's attorney.

106. What kinds of subjects may be discussed in a closed session with the public body's attorney?

Most obviously, the public body and its attorney may discuss claims made by or against the public body or litigation to which the public body or the local government is or may be a party. But the discussion is not limited to litigation; rather, the exception permits a public body to discuss any *legal* issue with its attorney. The attorney–client privilege does not cover nonlegal discussions between attorney and client. Thus a public body may not hold a closed session with its attorney to obtain his or her business or political advice.[68]

107. May the members of the public body discuss the legal issues presented by the attorney among themselves during the closed session with the attorney, or are they limited to hearing from the attorney and asking questions of the attorney?

The North Carolina Court of Appeals has made it clear that the board may discuss among themselves the legal issues presented by the attorney.[69]

---

68. *See* Multimedia Publ'g of N.C., Inc. v. Henderson Cty., 136 N.C. App. 567 (2000) (a public body may hold a closed session to discuss any legal matter with its attorney but it may not use such a closed session to discuss general policy matters); Gannett Pacific Corp. v. City of Asheville, 178 N.C. App. 711 (2006) (a board's closed sessions with its attorney, to hear reports about and give instructions for an ongoing mediation with another local government, were permissible as being within the attorney–client privilege); *In re* County of Erie, 473 F.3d 413 (2d Cir. 2007) (discussing how far policy advice can intrude into a lawyer's counsel to a governmental client yet still be protected by the privilege).

69. *See* Multimedia Publ'g of N.C., Inc. v. Henderson Cty., 145 N.C. App. 365 (2001).

108. May the public body give instructions to the attorney in closed sessions?

In some circumstances. The statute specifically permits the public body to "consider and give instructions" to the attorney concerning claims, litigation, and other legal proceedings. Other types of instructions, including those that will be communicated to a third party, may not be given in closed session. If the information is intended to be communicated to third parties, then it is not privileged. The public body may discuss these other sorts of potential instructions with the attorney in closed session, but the actual decision about what the instructions are must take place in an open session. For example, in *H.B.S. Contractors v. Cumberland County Board of Education*,[70] the school board, in closed session, instructed a school official to notify a contractor that the school board was terminating the contract. The court of appeals held that because the instruction was to be communicated to an outside party, it was not intended to be confidential and was therefore not within the attorney–client privilege. Because the action was not privileged, taking it in closed session violated the open meetings law.

109. What types of claims or litigation can be discussed? Does the exception apply only to suits before courts or does it also include actions before state or federal administrative agencies?

Quite clearly the latter. It applies to both judicial actions and administrative proceedings. The state court of appeals has said that the phrase "administrative procedure" in the statute means only state administrative proceedings undertaken pursuant to the state Administrative Procedure Act; but the court was not considering whether it also applied to federal administrative actions, and there is no basis in the statutory language for limiting the

---

70. 122 N.C. App. 49 (1996).

exception to state proceedings.[71] The exception also applies to proceedings before arbitrators or mediators.[72]

110. Does the action, proceeding, arbitration, or mediation have to be pending?

No. The law states specifically that a closed session may be held to discuss a claim against or on behalf of the body, which usually will not yet be the subject of a judicial action. Therefore, if the public body seeks advice from its attorney regarding a potential claim, even one that is not reasonably likely to occur, it may still meet in closed session to obtain that advice in order to preserve the attorney–client privilege.

111. A public body can discuss with its attorney its strategy for an arbitration or mediation in closed session. May the actual arbitration or mediation itself be held in a closed session if a majority of the members of the public body are present?

Not under the open meetings law. It clearly allows only discussion of strategy and the like, and participation must be limited to people within the attorney–client privilege. Thus, closed meetings among opposing parties would not be possible, even for purposes of negotiating or mediating a settlement. Several statutes, however, such as that requiring mediation of disputes between school boards and county commissioners, specifically exempt the actual arbitration or mediation between the statutorily defined working groups from open meetings requirements.[73] An alternative approach to mediation between public bodies is a system in which designated representatives (less than a majority) of each of

---

71. *See id.*

72. *Gannet Pacific Corp.*, 178 N.C. App. at 711.

73. See G.S. 115C-431(b), which exempts the proceedings of the working groups (defined in the statute) from the open meetings law requirements. Another such statute is G.S. 115C-238.29G(c), which excludes mediations between the State Board of Education and charter schools from the open meetings act.

two public boards participate in the mediation and report back to the whole board and the board attorney in a closed meeting. The North Carolina Court of Appeals held that this arrangement did not violate the open meetings law even though it was intentionally structured to avoid having the mediation occur in public.[74]

112. I have a couple of questions about the rule concerning settlements that are discussed in closed session. First, what if the other party to the lawsuit wants to seal the settlement? Can that be done?

No. The statute requires that the terms of the settlement be made public once it is final if it has been discussed in a closed session, and this requirement cannot be set aside by the litigants. Settlements are public under the public records law in any event.[75] A court can order or permit a settlement to be sealed upon a finding that "(1) the presumption of openness is overcome by an overriding interest and (2) . . . such overriding interest cannot be protected by any measure short of sealing the settlement."[76]

---

74. In *Gannett Pacific Corp.*, 178 N.C. App. at 711, a city and county were engaged in a mediation. During the course of a day-long mediation, each governing board held a number of closed sessions with its attorney to discuss the progress of the mediation and give instructions for further mediation sessions. The actual mediation involved the attorney for each board, along with one member of each board; these four met with the mediator.

75. G.S. 132-1.3 declares that all settlement documents in actions against the state of North Carolina or any political subdivision of the state are public record (with the exception of settlements in medical malpractice actions). In addition, the court of appeals has held that any settlement entered into by a state or local agency is a public record, regardless of whether the agency is plaintiff or defendant. News & Observer Publ'g Co. v. Wake Cty. Sys., 55 N.C. App. 1 (1981).

76. G.S. 132-1.3(b). A court order issued under this provision must articulate the overriding interest and include findings of fact sufficiently specific to permit a reviewing court to determine whether the order was proper.

113.   Okay, but what if the settlement is to be paid entirely with insurance proceeds, so that there is no public money involved. Can a settlement be sealed in that circumstance?

The answer is still no. If the settlement is discussed in closed session and if it binds the public body, then it must be made public regardless of the source of any money payments made on the public body's behalf.

114.   One other twist. What if the settlement is reported to the public body in closed session, but the public body does not discuss the settlement? Must the settlement be entered into the minutes?

Yes. If a proposed settlement is the occasion for a closed session, the terms of that settlement must be reported to and entered into the minutes of an open session.[77]

115.   The answer to Question 87 states that all board members are entitled to attend a closed session. What happens when a board member has sued the unit or the public body? Must that board member be allowed to attend closed sessions to discuss the lawsuit?

This is a difficult problem. In at least one state, the courts have held that participation by such a board member would violate common law rules against conflicts of interest, and therefore the board was allowed to exclude the board member.[78] It is not clear, however, that the common law has that strength in North Carolina. Some public bodies have appointed litigation committees that include all board members except the member who has sued, and

---

77. G.S. 143-318.11(a)(3). The statute requires the terms of a settlement to be reported to the public body and entered into its minutes "as soon as possible within a reasonable time after the settlement is concluded." This provision exempts malpractice settlements, which are not public records under G.S. 132-1.3(a).

78. *See* Scotch Plains–Fanwood Bd. of Educ. v. Syvertsen, 598 A.2d 1232 (N.J. Super. Ct. App. Div. 1991).

delegated the handling of any suits to these committees. Because the member who sued was not a member of the litigation committee, the committee could exclude him or her from its meetings.

Industry and Business Location and Expansion (G.S. 143-318.11(a)(4))

116. What does the exception for industrial or business location or expansion permit?

It permits the discussion in closed session of matters relating to the location or expansion of industries or of other businesses in the area served by the public body.[79]

117. Does the statute allow a general discussion of economic development policy in closed session?

Although the language of the statute might be read to permit such a discussion, the clear purpose of this exception is to permit discussion of particular industries or businesses. For that reason a court might read the language narrowly, so that a general discussion of policy would not be permissible.

118. May representatives of the industry or business be present at the closed session?

Yes. This sort of closed session is held primarily to protect the privacy of the company to which incentives might be offered. In this situation there is no privilege that might be compromised because of the presence of these outside parties.

119. May a board take action in such a closed session?

The statute specifically allows the board to agree on a tentative list of incentives to be offered to a company and to communicate that to the company. Final action approving the signing of an economic

---

79. A more extensive discussion of closed sessions under this exception is presented in David M. Lawrence, Economic Development Law for North Carolina Local Governments 90–94 (2000).

development contract or authorizing the payment of economic development expenditures must be taken in open session.[80]

120. Are discussions under this exception limited to projects authorized in the economic development statute (G.S. 158-7.1)?

No. Nothing in the statute nor in case law suggests such a limitation. The exception allows the public body to discuss any matter related to the location or expansion of industries and businesses in the area served by the public body.

Property Acquisition (G.S. 143-318.11(a)(5))

121. What about the exception for real property acquisition? What does it permit?

It permits a public body to consider and establish the public body's or the unit's negotiating position with respect to price and other material terms of any contract to acquire real property. The terms in question must be under negotiation with the seller of the property.[81]

122. Does real property acquisition include leases, easements, or other interests less than full ownership?

Probably. A lease or an easement is an interest in real property, and the policy reasons behind this exception apply as much to the negotiations for these lesser interests as they do to negotiations to acquire full ownership.

---

80. G.S. 143-318.11(a)(4). Additional procedural requirements for final approval of incentives are set forth in G.S. 158-7.1.

81. *See* Boney Publishers, Inc. v. Burlington City Council, 151 N.C. App. 651 (2002).

123. May the public body discuss whether to accept a gift of real property under this exception?

No. The statute permits the closed session when the property will be acquired by "purchase, option, exchange, or lease." A gift does not fit within the statutory language.

124. What about discussing the acquisition of property by eminent domain?

Such an acquisition doesn't fit within the statutory language either, but a public body will be able to discuss legal issues involving an eminent domain action in closed session under the exception that permits privileged conversations with the public body's attorney. See Questions 101–115.

125. May a board of county commissioners hold a closed session under this provision to review, for purposes of approval, the price that a local board of education plans to pay for a parcel of real property?

No. G.S. 115C-426(f) provides that a school board may not execute a contract for purchase of a school site unless the county commissioners have approved the price to be paid for the site. The commissioners are not negotiating the terms of such a contract but merely approving them, and therefore such a meeting does not fall within the statutory language.

126. What information does the public have a right to know regarding property that is the subject of a closed meeting under this exception?

The statute does not set out any special disclosure requirements for this category of closed session. A North Carolina Court of Appeals case held that information about property acquisition not related to the price or other material terms of the contract must be provided to the public if requested. In *Boney Publishers,*

Inc. v. Burlington City Council,[82] the city received a request for information relating to a planned closed session under the property acquisition authority. The information requested was (1) the property's current owner, (2) the property's location, and (3) the use or uses to which the public body intended to put the property. The court held that none of this information related to material terms of the contract and therefore could not be the subject of a closed session discussion. Although the case does not require release of the information absent a request, public bodies often provide it by including it on the agenda or in the motion to go into the closed session, or by disclosing it in some other fashion immediately before the closed session is held. In the rare case in which one of these items is actually under negotiation, there is no requirement to disclose information about that particular item.

127. May a local government in closed session instruct the person who is negotiating on its behalf for the property, or give instructions to an agent who will bid on its behalf for property being sold at auction?

Yes. The statute specifically permits the governing body to instruct its agents as to its negotiating position.

128. May a public body authorize the purchase itself in closed session?

Apparently so. Again, the statute permits giving instructions to a negotiator on behalf of the public body or unit. If the seller is willing to convey the property on terms acceptable to the public body, as communicated to the agent, it seems clear that the agent can go ahead and enter a contract to purchase on behalf of the public body.

---

82. 151 N.C. App. 651 (2002).

129. May a public body use a closed session to select the real property it wishes to purchase?

No. Previously the law specifically allowed closed sessions "to consider the selection of a site," but that language was deleted in 1994. The remaining authorization—to establish and instruct agents concerning the public body's position on price and other terms of purchase—is not broad enough to include discussions of which parcel of property to acquire, except in the rare case when that might be a subject of negotiation with a seller.[83]

130. What if the public body is considering properties in connection with a business or industry location or expansion? Can the public body discuss multiple properties in closed session and keep this information confidential?

Possibly, but perhaps only if it meets in closed session under the exception for discussing matters relating to the location or expansion of business or industries. This exception allows consideration of acquisition of property to use as an incentive for an economic development project, so it provides separate authority for such a discussion and probably allows the public body to withhold the information about the properties under consideration, at least until a final decision is made to acquire the property.[84] This option

---

83. *See* Tanque Verde Unified Sch. Dist. No. 13 of Pima Cty. v. Bernini, 76 P.3d 874, 882 (Ariz. Ct. App. 2003) (The Arizona open meetings statute permitted a closed session to allow the public body to "consider its position and instruct its representatives regarding negotiations for the purchase, sale or lease of real property." The court held that the quoted language did not permit a board to hold a closed session to select a site.).

84. See Op. Att'y Gen. (February 13, 1995), http://www.ncdoj.gov/About-DOJ/Legal-Services/Legal-Opinions/Opinions/Open-Meetings-Law;-Closed-Meetings-to-Discuss-Acqu.aspx, and "Acquiring real property for redevelopment—can local governments keep it confidential?", Tyler Mulligan, *Coates' Canons: Local Government Law Blog*, http://canons.sog.unc.edu/acquiring-real-property-for-redevelopment-can-local-governments-keep-it-confidential/. Prior to acquiring

is available only if the property is being considered for a particular business or industry. The language of the business and industry exception does not support holding a closed session to decide among properties for a speculative economic development project.

131. Aside from the incentive situation, is there any way to protect information about a public entity's interest in acquiring a particular property?

Perhaps so. The purpose of the exception is to protect a discussion among a majority of the public body. Nothing in the law prohibits the body from delegating to an employee or contracted agent authority for initial identification of properties and preliminary negotiations. Such a delegation could include a price range and other criteria (all of which would be public information). Under this authority the employee or other agent could proceed with a tentative agreement, which could be reviewed by the board in closed session (the information about the specific property, as described in Question 126, would have to be disclosed if requested). Final approval or rejection would have to occur in open session; however, counter-offers or negotiations on terms to be communicated through the agent could be approved in closed session.

132. So much for real property acquisition. May a public body hold a closed session to discuss the disposal of real property?

No. There is no authorization for discussing property disposition in closed session. State statutes require, in most cases, that real property be sold by competitive or private sale procedures, requiring public notice.[85]

---

property for economic development, however, the governing body would have to hold a public hearing under G.S. 158-7.1(c).

85. See Article 12 of G.S. Chapter 160A, applicable to counties under G.S. 153A-176.

133. What about an exchange of real property?

If a local government is considering an exchange in which the unit would acquire real property, it may be that much of the discussion can be held in closed session.

134. Does the law ever permit a closed session with regard to acquiring personal property?

No.

Personnel Matters and Employment Contracts (G.S. 143-318.11(a)(5), (6))

135. The exceptions for personnel matters are probably the ones that are used most often. What is authorized under these provisions?

The statute permits closed sessions for three general types of personnel-related matters. First, a public body may consider and establish its negotiating position regarding the compensation and other terms in any employment contract.[86] Second, a public body may consider the "qualifications, competence, performance, character, fitness, conditions of appointment, or conditions of initial employment" of a present or prospective public officer or employee.[87] Third, it may hear or investigate a complaint, charge, or grievance either by or against an officer or employee.[88]

136. Does an "employment contract" include contracts with the public body's retained attorney or with other independent professionals?

No. It only includes contracts with employees, and a retained attorney is not an employee of the unit but, rather, an independent contractor. Independent contractors are not employees of the entity with which they contract, so their contracts are not covered by this exception.

---

86. G.S. 143-318.11(a)(5)(ii).
87. G.S. 143-318.11(a)(6).
88. *Id.*

137.   May the public body give instructions in closed session about negotiating an employment contract?

Yes. That is expressly permitted.

138.   The second general type of personnel-related discussion seems to be the broadest. May this exception be used to discuss general personnel policies?

No. It is available only for talking about specific individuals.

139.   If a public body wishes to use this exception, must the officer or employee in question be one who is appointed by the body?

No. The exception is available to discuss any public officer or employee (with the few exceptions noted below), whether appointed by the public body or by some other person or body.[89]

140.   What about elected officials who are full-time employees— could a board of county commissioners discuss the performance of the sheriff or register of deeds in closed session?

Not under the exception in G.S. 143-318.11(a)(6) as it applies to employees, but perhaps as it applies to applicants or public officers. The North Carolina Supreme Court has held that elected sheriffs and registers of deeds, and their employees, are not county employees for purposes of G.S. 153A-99 (limiting political activities and coercion of public employees).[90] The Supreme Court has also held, however, that records of applicants to fill a vacancy for the office of sheriff are confidential under the county personnel privacy statute, G.S. 153A-98.[91] Why the different outcome? The court held that "[t]he clear purpose of [the personnel privacy

---

89. *See* Camden Cty. v. Haddock, 523 S.E.2d 291 (Ga. 1999) (reaching this result under a statute comparable to North Carolina's).

90. *See* Young v. Bailey, 781 S.E.2d 277, 280 (N.C. 2016) (sheriffs) and Sims-Campbell v. Welch, 769 S.E.2d 643 (N.C. 2015) (registers of deeds).

91. Durham Herald Co. v. Cty. of Durham, 334 N.C. 677 (1993).

statute] is to provide some confidentiality to those who apply to county boards or their agents for positions which those boards and their agents are authorized to fill."[92] Since boards of county commissioners have the authority to fill vacancies in the offices of the sheriff and the register of deeds, they likely have authority to discuss applicants for appointment in closed session under the provision designed to prevent the disclosure of confidential records. In addition, the register of deeds, the sheriff, and the sworn officers in the sheriff's office may also be the subject of a closed session because of their status as public officers.

141. May a public body hold a closed session to discuss the performance of volunteers, such as members of a publicly funded rescue squad?

That's a complicated question without a clear answer. The statute permits closed sessions for discussions about employees only, and unpaid volunteers are not employees. If volunteers are given nominal compensation, however, as is often the case with rescue squad workers, volunteer firefighters, and some sorts of recreation workers, the Internal Revenue Service considers them employees for tax purposes. These small payments do not turn the volunteers into employees in other contexts, though. They are not considered employees, for example, under the Local Government Employees Retirement System. So, we can't be sure how a court would treat them for purposes of discussions in closed session.

---

92. *Durham Herald Co.*, 334 at 679 ("An 'applicant' holds no position with the county whether as an 'employee' in the strict sense of the term or as an elected public official such as the sheriff. He, or she, is merely an applicant for such positions. It is as applicants that the statute seeks to afford them and their applications some measure of confidentiality.").

142.   Can this exception be used to discuss the salary of an individual employee?

Yes. Such discussions will inevitably involve considerations of the qualifications, competence, character, fitness, and performance of an employee, and salary is a condition of employment.

143.   What about using it to consider the size of the pay raise to be given to employees generally?

No. Such a discussion concerns general personnel policies and not specific individuals. As Question 138 notes, the exception permits only discussion of specific individuals.

144.   Can a public body actually set a person's salary in closed session?

The answer to this question is not entirely clear. Nothing in the open meetings law specifically requires a public body to make decisions about a specific employee's salary in open session. And, as already noted, the law allows discussion about individual salaries to occur in closed session. On the other hand, a public employee's actual salary is public information, and there is no specific authority to make this decision in closed session. A public body probably may approve a proposed salary—for example, one that will be offered to an employee as part of a retention effort. In that situation the salary is not final and would likely be considered confidential personnel information unless and until it is actually implemented.[93] In addition, the public body probably has authority to reach a tentative consensus about a specific salary in closed session prior to taking final action in open session.[94]

---

93. The compensation of some public hospital employees is confidential under G.S. 131E-257.2. Therefore a closed session to discuss performance and set salaries is authorized under the exception to protect confidential information.

94. See Question 96 (citing Maready v. City of Winston-Salem, 342 N.C. 708 (1996)).

145. May a public body hold a closed session to discuss its relationship with its chief administrator, as when a city council discusses relations with the city manager?

Yes. Such a discussion concerns the performance of a public employee, the chief administrator.

146. If the public body is discharging an employee, such as a county or city manager, may it discuss or decide on a severance package in closed session?

Not under the exception for personnel. A discussion about severance normally doesn't concern the performance or qualifications of the employee being discharged. Indeed, a lack of legal consideration usually prohibits the award of severance to an employee who is already under contract. If the severance is part of the negotiation of an initial contract, the discussion can occur in closed session under either the contract negotiation or the personnel exception. Furthermore, in some circumstances there may be a threat of litigation by the employee, and a severance package might be discussed as part of settling the underlying dispute or consulting with the attorney regarding the legality of the proposed payments.

147. What about a discussion of an individual board member's performance, or about the board's relationship within itself—that is, how the members work together and how they might improve?

The statute specifically prohibits closed sessions to talk about the performance of members of the public body itself. Two other exceptions might apply, however, in particular situations. In the case of an allegation of criminal activity by a board member, the board could consider the matter under the exception in G.S. 143-318.11(a)(7): "to plan, conduct, or hear reports concerning investigations of alleged criminal conduct." In addition, the board may meet in closed session to obtain information or advice from its attorney about legal issues and options regarding the board member's behavior.

148. Does this mean that, except for legal questions, a discussion about whether to censure a board member, and a vote on whether to do so, must all occur in open session?

Yes.

149. What if a citizen or employee has a complaint or grievance about the actions of a member of the public body?

The board may be able to hear and gather information about such a grievance in closed session. The statute authorizes a public body to meet in closed session to "hear or investigate a complaint, charge, or grievance by or against a specific public officer or employee." So the prohibition on considering the performance, qualifications, character, and fitness of members of the public body in a closed session may not preclude the public body from *hearing a grievance* against a member in closed session. The public body would, however, have to discuss the substance of the grievance in open session and would have to take any action, such as censure, in open session as well.[95]

150. One more variation: What about a discussion of the performance, whether individually or collectively, of the members of another board, including one appointed by the public body?

The statute specifically prohibits closed sessions held to talk about the performance of members of other public bodies.

---

95. The discussion in the text corresponds with the advice of the North Carolina Attorney General's office to the chair of the ethics committee of the North Carolina House of Representatives concerning an investigation of charges against a member of the House. Op. Att'y Gen. (September 25, 1995), http://www.ncdoj.gov/About-DOJ/Legal-Services/Legal-Opinions/Opinions/Open-Meetings;-Public-Records.aspx.

151.   The statute explicitly requires some personnel actions to be taken in open session. What are they?

The personnel exception expressly requires that a "final action making an appointment or discharge or removal by a public body having final authority for the appointment or discharge or removal" must come in open session.

152.   I have a specific question about the meaning of "appointment" in the public school context. Certainly, when a school superintendent is first hired, that's an appointment; but what about extending the superintendent's contract for a second or later term?

That's a close question, but extending a superintendent's contract is essentially reappointing the official, and a court would likely consider the contract extension to be an "appointment." The vote to extend should come in open session.

153.   What about a school board that decides not to renew the superintendent's contract? In that case the board is simply letting a contract end. Would that be considered a "discharge or removal"?

A decision not to offer a new contract to a superintendent ends the board's employment relationship with that officer and should be treated the same as a discharge. (Remember, only the action itself has to occur in open session; the entire discussion preceding that point can take place in closed session.)

154.   Are there any personnel actions that may be taken in closed session?

The express statutory language quoted in Question 151 implies that certain other actions might be taken in closed session. Two sorts of actions come to mind. First, a public body might take some action other than an appointment or discharge in closed session. For example, it might take action to suspend an employee or vote to recommend to the manager that an employee be disciplined.[96] As noted in Question 144, the board might also approve in closed session a tentative or proposed salary change or promotion for a particular employee. Indeed, with respect to any personnel action that involves information that is not public, the board may be legally obligated to take action in closed session to protect information that is confidential under the personnel privacy statutes.

155. I have a question about the phrase "final action making . . . [a] discharge." Could a board vote in closed session to ask for the resignation of the manager? That's not a discharge; rather, the manager resigns.

A literal reading of the statute suggests that a board may reach consensus to remove an employee, but it may also exercise its discretion to allow the employee to resign rather than be discharged. Since only the final action making the discharge must be made in open session, perhaps the statute allows a board to agree in closed session to refrain from taking that action if the employee prefers to resign. (This has significance under the public records law, which makes public information about a dismissal for disciplinary reasons, but does not require release of information about resignation, other than the fact that a person has resigned.) On the other hand, a court might conclude that when a board agrees to ask for an employee's resignation, it has in effect made a final decision to terminate the employee, and therefore such a decision must be made in open session.

---

96. *See* Jeske v. Upper Yoder Twp., 403 A.2d 1010 (Pa. Commw. Ct. 1979) (The Pennsylvania open meetings law permits a board to "consider dismissal" of an employee in closed session. The court held that a board could act in closed session to suspend an employee, pending a public hearing on the employee's possible dismissal, because such an action was part of the consideration of the dismissal.).

156.   What about a public body that does not have final authority for appointment or discharge? What authority does that body have to take action in a closed session on a personnel matter?

A public body without final authority for an appointment or discharge might vote to recommend a specific appointment or discharge to the body or person with that final authority. For example, a city planning commission might, in closed session, interview candidates and recommend a specific candidate for city planning director to the city manager, who has the power to make the appointment. Similarly, the governing board in a council–manager form of government might act to recommend that the manager terminate the police chief.

157.   County boards of elections nominate their candidate for county elections director and send that name to the state elections director, who issues a letter of appointment. Who has final authority to make the appointment?

Probably the county board of elections. The state elections director is understood not to have any power to reject the county board's nominee. Therefore, the county board of elections should decide upon its nominee in open session.

158.   What about holding a closed session to establish the qualifications for a position about to be filled, to establish the procedure for filling the position, or other matters of that sort?

This is not authorized. Such a discussion is about the character-istics of a position or the details of a procedure rather than about any specific individual who fills the position. The same would be true of discussing the advertisement for the position or deciding upon interview questions to ask of applicants.

159.   Does the exception permit a closed session to consider or fill a vacancy on the board itself?

No. The law specifically forbids filling or even considering such a vacancy in the public body's membership in closed session.

160. Does that prohibition apply when some other board fills the vacancy? In our community, advisory boards such as the planning board often make recommendations to the governing board when there is a vacancy on the advisory board.

The prohibition applies to the advisory board as well. The statute prohibits any board from meeting in closed session to consider a vacancy in its own membership, and therefore such an advisory board could not, in closed session, consider whom to recommend to the governing board for appointment to the advisory board.

161. What about when a city council is considering or filling a vacancy in the office of mayor? After all, under the general law the mayor is not a member of the public body, and in the answer to Question 29 the mayor was not counted in determining the number of persons needed to hold an official meeting.

Despite that, the prohibition on discussing vacancies in closed sessions almost certainly applies to vacancies in the office of the mayor. There is a basic presumption in the law toward openness, and the policies behind the two provisions suggest that the mayor shall be included in one and not in the other. The answer to Question 29 argued that if a mayor votes only to break ties, a majority of the board—not counting the nonvoting mayor—would be sufficient to trigger the notice requirements under the open meetings law, even though it is not sufficient to constitute a quorum. In that case, the interpretation is consistent with the purpose of preventing a functional majority from meeting outside of the public eye. With the closed session provision, the act's policy cuts in a different direction. The only public bodies at the local level that fill their own vacancies are city councils, boards of county commissioners, and local school boards. Each of these is an elected governing board. In a real sense, then, the principal thrust of the prohibition is a prohibition on considering or filling vacancies on elected governing boards in closed session. Even if the mayor is not technically a member of the council, he or she does preside at council meetings and votes in case of a tie and therefore is effectively a member of the governing board. The statutory policy applies as much to mayoral vacancies as it does to council vacancies. This provision should thus be understood to include a vacancy in the office of presiding officer of the public body, even if that presiding officer is not, in all contexts, a member of the public body.

162. Would those same considerations suggest that the prohibition also applies to a board while it is considering and choosing a presiding officer from among its own members?

Yes, they do. In addition, the statute prohibits considering the qualifications and competence of members of the public body, and those considerations are part of the decision-making process in selecting a presiding officer.

163. Does the prohibition apply to a public body's discussions about appointments to other boards and commissions?

Yes. The statute specifically prohibits closed sessions for this purpose.

164. Who has the right to decide whether a personnel discussion, one clearly within the exception, is open or closed— the public body or the person being discussed?

Under the statute, the public body decides, even though it is generally the employee's interests that the exception seeks to protect. In the case of a disciplinary hearing, some courts have held that employees enjoy a constitutional right to an open hearing, should they request it.[97] But the United States Fourth Circuit Court of Appeals (the Fourth Circuit includes North Carolina, and its decisions are therefore binding on federal courts in this state on matters of federal law) has denied any such right to the employee.[98] Therefore, a public body could, at present, keep such a hearing closed against the employee's wishes.

---

97. *See, e.g.,* Fitzgerald v. Hampton, 467 F.2d 755 (D.C. Cir. 1972).

98. Satterfield v. Edenton–Chowan Bd. of Educ., 530 F.2d 567 (4th Cir. 1975).

165. Can a public body discuss independent contractors, such as its planning consultants or engineering firms, in closed session?

No. Before 1994 there was an exception in the open meetings law for discussions of the performance of independent contractors, but it was deleted by amendments enacted that year. Because independent contractors are neither officers nor employees of the local government, their reputation or performance may not be discussed under the personnel exception. Therefore, unless the discussion involves a legal issue to be addressed under the attorney–client privilege, a public body may not hold a closed session to discuss independent contractors or their employment or discharge.

166. Can the performance of a local government's attorney be discussed in closed session when the attorney is in private practice?

That's unclear. The statute permits discussion of the performance of public officers and employees. An attorney in private practice is not an employee of the local government, but whether that attorney is an officer is unclear. The court of appeals has characterized a county or city attorney as a public officer in some contexts, but that doesn't mean the attorney is an officer in all contexts.[99] On the other hand, if the county or city attorney is considered to hold a public office, these attorneys would be subject to the rules on holding multiple offices, which may create a problem for a number of attorneys who represent three or more local governments.[100]

---

99. *See* City of Winston-Salem v. Yarbrough, 117 N.C. App. 340 (1994) (the court characterized the city attorney as a public officer for liability purposes); Womack Newspapers, Inc. v. Town of Kitty Hawk, 181 N.C. App. 1 (2007) (contract attorney is a public officer; thus, documents held by a contract attorney were public records.).

100. *See* G.S. 128-1 (limiting public officers to two appointive offices.).

167.   You also mentioned that a board may hold a closed session to hear a complaint or grievance against a public officer or employee. How does that apply when a citizen wants to make such a charge during the public comment portion of the board's meeting?

If a citizen wishes to use his or her public comment time to offer a complaint or grievance, the public body may certainly move into closed session to hear the matter. The term *"public* comment" refers to the rights of members of the public to address the board and does not imply that such comments must always be heard in open session. On the other hand, even though most information gathered about employees is confidential under the personnel privacy exception to the public records law, nothing prohibits a citizen from airing complaints about employees or officers in open session, and the public body is not required to hear such complaints in closed session.

Other Closed Session Purposes

168.   Under what circumstances does the exception for investigations (G.S. 143-318.11(a)(7)) apply?

It is fairly narrow, since it applies only to investigations of alleged criminal conduct. With regard to such an investigation, however, a public body may plan it, conduct it, and hear reports concerning it in closed session.[101]

---

101. *See* Rhode Island Affiliate, ACLU v. Bernasconi, 557 A.2d 1232 (R.I. 1989) (open meetings law that permits closed sessions concerning investigations of alleged criminal misconduct interpreted to allow a closed session at which a local school board approved drug searches of student lockers).

169. What is involved with the exceptions for school violence response plans and anti-terrorism plans (G.S. 143-318.11(a)(8), (9))?

These narrow exceptions permit (1) local school boards to hold closed sessions to formulate plans and emergency responses to deal with school violence incidents and (2) any public body to hold a closed session to receive briefings and to discuss and take action to protect public safety as it relates to terrorist activity.

170. How might a local government use the exception for honors, awards, and scholarships?

That exception (G.S. 143-318.11(a)(2)) is designed to prevent the premature disclosure of an honorary degree, scholarship, prize, or award. It permits holding closed sessions to select recipients for honors and awards and is of most use to the university system. It has occasionally been used by local governments that wish to make an award to a long-time employee, recognize local citizens, or name a building after a donor.

171. What about consideration of auditor's reports? Auditors sometimes prefer to discuss their management letters in closed session.

No exception permits closed sessions for this specific purpose.

172. You haven't mentioned any exception that permits closed sessions to consider contract negotiations in general.

There isn't one. The statute specifically permits closed sessions for developing negotiating positions for real estate purchase and employment contracts, but that is all; there is no provision related to contract issues in general. A public body could consider legal issues arising within a contract negotiation in closed session under the attorney–client exception, but it could not then use that session to develop business strategies for the contract negotiation.

Disclosure of Closed Session Information

173. If a board holds a closed session, may it prohibit its members from disclosing what happened at the session?

Probably not. The open meetings law does not itself address this question. However, the permission to hold a closed session is simply a permission to exclude the public; it is not an authorization to prohibit those present from disclosing what occurred. What little case law there is suggests that if a public body sought to enforce such a prohibition, such as by censuring or attempting to suspend a member, it might be violating that member's constitutional rights of free speech.[102] Individual board members may be liable for disclosing information discussed in a closed session under other laws, however. For example, the personnel privacy and trade secret provisions prohibit release of information and provide sanctions for violations of those restrictions.

174. So if reporters learn what happened at a closed session, there is nothing to prevent them reporting on the session?

That's right, again, as long as there is no other legal prohibition on releasing the information.

175. Well, can members of the public body sign a confidentiality agreement, under which they agree not to disclose what happened at a closed session?

Certainly, as long as it's understood they are signing as *individuals*. They can't promise confidentiality on behalf of the *public body* since the statute itself requires, in most cases, that the minutes and general account of any closed session be made public. These types of agreements are common in economic development situations, where a business or industry does not wish to disclose its identity until a final decision is made.

---

102. *See* Kucinich v. Forbes, 432 F. Supp. 1101 (N.D. Ohio 1977).

Exceptions for Particular Public Bodies

176. The answer to Question 78 mentioned that one type of local government body is completely excepted from the open meetings law. What is that exception?

The exception exempts from the statute all law enforcement agencies, which probably means all agencies whose officers enjoy the power of arrest.[103] The apparent purpose of the exception is to protect the secrecy of law enforcement investigations. As a practical matter, this exception may not be very important, since law enforcement agencies normally are not organized as boards, and what boards there are normally do not participate in investigations.

177. I thought there was some sort of exception for quasi-judicial agencies.

There is, but it applies only to agencies subject to the State Executive Budget Act—that is, only to state agencies.[104] There is no general exception for local government quasi-judicial agencies, such as boards of adjustment. A public body may go into closed session to confer with its attorney, but its deliberations must occur in open session.

---

103. G.S. 143-318.18(5).

104. *See* G.S. 143-318.18(7). Another provision, G.S. 143-318.18(6), provides authority for state occupational licensing boards to undertake certain activities in closed session. Separate provisions in some of the occupational licensing board statutes also contain exceptions. *See, e.g.,* G.S. 90-16 (North Carolina Medical Board); G.S. 138A-12 (Deliberations of the State Ethics Commission).

Minutes and General Accounts

178. The statute requires public bodies to create minutes of all official meetings, and general accounts of closed sessions.[105] What's the difference between minutes and a general account?

The purpose of *minutes* is to provide a record of the actions taken by a board and evidence that the actions were taken according to proper procedures. If no action is taken, the minutes need only contain the information necessary to document that the meeting occurred.[106] If a closed session is held and no action is taken, then a statement, made in open session and recorded in the open meeting minutes, that "no action was taken" in the closed session, satisfies the legal requirement for minutes of that closed session. Apart from their legal purpose, minutes also provide a historical record of the work of a public body. For that reason, they typically include a summary of matters discussed. The public body has discretion in determining the amount of detail to include.

The purpose of a *general account*, on the other hand, is to provide some sort of record of the discussion that took place in the closed session, whether action was taken or not. A public body must always prepare a general account of a closed session, even if there are no actions to document in the minutes. As a practical matter, the general account of a meeting at which action is taken will usually serve as the minutes of that meeting as well, if the account includes a record of any actions taken.

---

105. G.S. 143-318.10(3). *See also* G.S. 153A-42 and 160A-72 (requiring the clerk to keep full and accurate minutes of county and city governing boards).

106. *See* Maready v. City of Winston-Salem, 342 N.C. 708 (1996). In this case, the state supreme court agreed with the characterization of minutes as set out in the answer to this question. It was this decision, in fact, that led the General Assembly to require the preparation of a general account of each closed session.

179. What specific information should be included in minutes when actions are taken? For example, do the minutes have to identify how members voted?

There is no general statutory requirement to identify who voted which way. County and city governing board members are required to record the results of the vote, and any member may request that the "ayes and noes" be taken on any particular action and recorded in the minutes.[107] There is a legal reason to be specific about the vote count in other situations, and to record other aspects of the vote in order to assess and verify the validity of the action. So, for example, it may not be sufficient for the minutes to say simply that a motion passed. If a subsequent challenge alleges that a vote of more than a majority was required, there would be no way to determine whether the vote was sufficient. Other information that could be necessary to determine whether an action was valid includes vacancies, members who have been excused from voting or who have abstained, members who have left the meeting (and whether they were excused from the meeting before they left), and members who are participating remotely.

180. How detailed must a general account of a closed session be?

The open meetings law requires that general accounts must be created "so that a person not in attendance would have a reasonable understanding of what transpired."[108] The state court of appeals has had one case in which it reviewed a general account prepared by a board of county commissioners, and it held that the general account satisfied the statutory requirement. In that case the general account specified each stage of discussion in the closed session, but it did not summarize the substance of the discussion nor did it set out the specific positions taken by each member of

---

107. *See* G.S. 153A-42 and 160A-72.
108. G.S. 143-318.10(e).

the public body. The case offers, then, a useful model of an adequate general account.[109]

181. Are minutes or general accounts available for public inspection under the public records law?

Generally, yes, although there are some exceptions. The statute provides that minutes and general accounts are public records, but it also permits a public body to withhold them from public inspection for "so long as public inspection would frustrate the purpose of a closed session."[110]

182. Well, how long might that be?

That will depend on the content of the minutes or general account. If they record instructions to the manager to purchase a tract of land, they would be opened to public inspection once the contract of sale has been executed. On the other hand, if they reveal information about public assistance recipients, they should be kept sealed for as long as federal and state laws continue to require that public assistance records be kept confidential.

183. What about minutes of closed sessions regarding employees? Are those confidential personnel records?

Yes. They fit the definition of personnel records under the personnel privacy statutes, and according to a North Carolina Court of Appeals opinion, their release will always frustrate the purpose of a closed session.[111]

---

109. *See* Multimedia Publ'g of N.C., Inc. v. Henderson Cty., 145 N.C. App. 365 (2001).

110. G.S. 143-318.10(e).

111. Times News Publ'g Co. v. Alamance–Burlington Bd. of Educ., 774 S.E.2d 922, 927 (2015).

184. If the minutes need not be made public, how can they be approved by the public body?

The public body may hold a new closed session to approve the minutes of an earlier closed session. Doing so would "prevent the disclosure of information that is . . . confidential pursuant to the law of this State"—the first statutory authorization for a closed session.

185. How does a board that has sealed minutes or a general account of a closed session go about unsealing those documents?

The best practice is to designate those minutes that are to be sealed when they are approved. Some pubic bodies seal all minutes and general accounts and direct the public body's attorney (or some other official) to periodically review them and determine when they may be unsealed, and to respond to requests for access to specific minutes and general accounts on behalf of the public body. Increasingly, public bodies provide access to these records on their public websites. This provides a high level of transparency and requires the board or an employee with delegated authority to review to make a more timely ongoing assessment of what will be released to the public.

186. If one board seals the minutes or general account of a closed session, could a later board order that they be unsealed?

Sure. The statute provides that minutes and general accounts of closed sessions are public records. This means that a board must release them, upon request, unless there is justification for continuing to withhold them. This obligation is binding on the board regardless of when the closed session occurred. In the absence of a specific request, the decision to unseal general accounts is within the discretion of the board. No board can bind a successor board on a matter of discretion. Of course if a statute, such as the confidential-record statutes noted in Question 99, requires that certain minutes remain confidential, no board has the discretion to release them.

187. Speaking of old boards and new boards, can a board member vote on the approval of minutes of a meeting the member did not attend?

Yes. A local government board is considered to be a continuous body, even though the individuals who serve on it change over time. The former board members no longer have authority to approve the minutes and the new members do. Indeed, the new members *should* do so, unless they have specific, reliable information or evidence that the minutes are not accurate.

188. What if a new board member objects to the decisions documented in the minutes of the old board?

Approval of the minutes is not an approval of what was done in the meeting. It simply confirms that the minutes are an accurate record of what took place. New board members should be able to rely on the clerk and the incumbent members to vouch for the accuracy of minutes in these situations.

189. Say a person was a member of a public body at the time it held a closed session. Does that person have a right to look at the sealed minutes or general account of the closed session once he or she is no longer a member?

No. Once such a person has concluded service on the public body, he or she has no greater rights of access to nonpublic records than does any other citizen.

190. What about current members of the public body? Does each of them have a right to examine closed session minutes?

Perhaps not, as individuals. The minutes belong to the board as a whole and not to its separate members. A majority of the board could adopt a policy allowing individuals to have access upon request, or it could reserve the right to approve individual requests for access. It could also allow inspection only at meetings of the public body. The power of the board to limit access, however, may not be absolute. If a board member was unable to attend a closed session, or requires access to minutes in order to become informed about a pending matter, the member may have an argument that the board is required to provide access to the minutes, and that denial deprives the member of information necessary to discharge the duties of the office.[112]

191. Sometimes an individual board member wants his or her comments to be included in the minutes, or requests that the clerk revise minutes to include the individual's preferred language. Must the clerk make these changes for each individual board member who requests them?

No. The minutes and general accounts belong to the board and the board, not an individual member, determines their content. A board could adopt a policy allowing individual board members to dictate the content, but such a process could be difficult for the clerk to manage.

192. Is it legal to use sound or video recordings of meetings as minutes and general accounts?

Yes, the statute specifically allows this.[113] An advantage of this approach is that it provides a complete record of everything said and done at the meeting. It is not a practical approach, however, for several reasons. First, recordings are more difficult to search for specific information. In addition, minutes and general accounts must be retained permanently. Changes in audio and video technology will likely require recordings to be transferred to a more durable format.[114]

---

112. *See* ANN TAYLOR SCHWING, OPEN MEETING LAWS § 5.58 (3d ed. 2011); Gabrilson v. Flynn, 554 N.W.2d 267, 275 (Iowa 1996) ("Members of the school board are granted policy making power and to adequately exercise that power, we hold that they generally should be allowed access to both public and private records that are necessary for the proper discharge of their duties.").

113. G.S. 143-318.10(e).

114. *See* G.S. 132-8.2.

193.   What about a recording of a closed session that is used to prepare the minutes? Is it a public record and, if so, how long must be it retained?

These recordings are public records, but they may be withheld if release would frustrate the purpose of the closed session. Indeed, some will be confidential under exceptions to the public records law. Under state records retention requirements, they may be erased once the minutes or general account is prepared and approved, just as tapes made of open sessions may be destroyed once the minutes are prepared and approved.

194.   Does an individual board member have a right to record a closed session for that member's own purposes?

Probably not. While the open meetings law allows any person to record an open session (see Question 207), there is no such authority for closed sessions. Individual board members, or others who attend closed sessions, may wish to create a recording for their own use. This often happens, unfortunately, when there is a lack of trust among members of the public body. No North Carolina statute or case addresses this question, but the board probably has authority to decide whether an individual member can record a closed session. Such a recording, if released, would in effect allow one member unilaterally to reverse the board's decision to meet in closed session. A board member may argue that state law allows such a recording. G.S. 15A-287 prohibits the secret recording of communications, but allows it if one party to the conversation consents. While this law clarifies that a person does not commit a crime by secretly recording a closed session, nothing in that statute creates a right to record a conversation in any particular context. A rule prohibiting individual recordings would likely fall within the broad authority of local governing boards to adopt rules governing the conduct of their meetings.[115] Cases from other states

---

115. *See* G.S. 153A-41 (counties); G.S. 160A-71(c) (cities).

have recognized local government boards' authority to prohibit a member from recording closed sessions.[116]

195. How would a board enforce a policy prohibiting an individual board member from recording a closed session?

That's not entirely clear. There is no specific authority to remove a board member from a meeting unless the member "willfully interrupts, disturbs, or disrupts" the meeting.[117] A federal court case arising out the town of East Spencer, North Carolina, held that police officers had probable cause to remove a board member after a disruption occurred over the member's refusal to comply with the board's policy prohibiting taping of a closed session.[118]

Aspects of Public Access

196. The open meetings law says that "any person" is entitled to attend official meetings of public bodies. Does that mean that a public body must accommodate every single person who wants to attend a meeting?

No, but the public body must take "reasonable measures to provide access." This standard comes from the North Carolina Court of Appeals opinion in *Garlock v. Wake County Board of Education*, in which the court rejected the notion that the "any person" language literally creates an obligation to accommodate everyone who wishes to attend. Citing a national treatise on open meetings laws,

---

116. *See* Dean v. Guste, 414 So. 2d 862 (La. App. 1982) (upholding a school board's policy and holding that members have no First Amendment right to record meetings); Zamora v. Edgewood Indep. Sch. Dist., 592 S.W.2d 649 (Texas App. 1980).

117. *See* G.S.143-318.17 (failure to comply with a request to leave in this situation constitutes a misdemeanor).

118. King v. Jefferies, 402 F. Supp. 2d 624 (M.D.N.C. 2005) (the case involves claims arising out of the forcible removal of the plaintiff and did not rule on the legality of the prohibition on taping).

the court noted that the intent of the "any person" language may best be interpreted as preventing a public body from allowing only certain categories of persons and excluding others from a public meeting. Under this reasoning, "*any* person may attend, meaning that attendance may not be limited to *a particular classification or group of people.*"[119] The court concluded that the open meetings law is satisfied as long as the public body takes "reasonable measures" to accommodate members of the public, even if some of them are not actually able to attend.[120]

197. Does the open meetings law give citizens a right to address the public body holding the open meeting?

No. The open meetings law gives persons a right to attend and observe the proceedings of a public body. It gives no right to address the public body or participate in its deliberations. Three types of public bodies, however—boards of county commissioners, city councils, and local boards of education—are subject to separate statutes that require them to provide a period for "public comment" in at least one meeting a month.[121] In addition, local governments are sometimes required to solicit public comment regarding specific matters in public hearings, as described in Questions 235–242.

---

119. 211 N.C. App. 200, 218 (2011) (citing ANN TAYLOR SCHWING & CONSTANCE TAYLOR, OPEN MEETING LAWS § 5.90 (1994)).

120. *Garlock*, 211 N.C. App. at 225, relying on Gutierrez v. City of Albuquerque, 631 P.2d 304 (N.M. 1981). *See also* Maxwell v. Carney, 548 S.E.2d 293 (Ga. 2001); State *ex rel.* Badke v. Village Bd., 494 N.W.2d 408 (Wis. 1993).

121. The statutes requiring a period for public comment are G.S. 153A-52.1 (boards of county commissioners), G.S. 160A-81.1 (city councils), and G.S. 115C-51 (local boards of education).

198. Does the open meetings law say anything about meeting rooms? If the room is too small for the audience, has there been a violation of the law?

The law says nothing about the size of meeting rooms, but it is possible to violate it by holding a meeting in a room that does not accommodate at least some members of the public. The *Garlock* case, discussed in Question 196, involved this issue. The court held that the public body was not legally obligated to relocate a meeting to a larger room in a different building to accommodate an expected larger-than-usual attendance. In the same case, however, the court held that it *was* a violation to hold a meeting in a small room, completely excluding members of the public because members of the governing body and its staff had used all the seating. The court held that larger rooms were available within the building, and the failure to use them was not reasonable. The court also noted that moving to a different building would require a new notice, whereas moving to another room in the same building would not. (The outcome, thus, might depend on the specificity of the notice.)

199. How does the provision of overflow space with live audiovisual coverage, or the provision of live coverage by the media, affect the public body's obligation to accommodate the public in the meeting room itself?

The *Garlock* case affirmed that provision of overflow space with live audiovisual feed is a reasonable way to provide access. In the case where the size of the room excludes all members of the public, however, the availability of third party media coverage was insufficient to overcome a violation of the open meetings law.[122]

---

122. *Garlock*, 211 N.C. App. at 227.

200. Can a public body use a ticketing system to manage a situation where a larger-than-normal crowd is expected?

Yes. The court in *Garlock* held that a ticketing system is a reasonable measure, so long as the notice of the meeting includes information about the ticket requirement.[123]

201. Does the open meetings law require a public body to make accommodations for a person who is disabled or has difficulty physically attending a meeting?

No. Other federal and state laws may require some accommodation, but the failure to comply with those requirements, or to accommodate such a person, does not violate the open meetings law.[124]

202. Can a public body hold a meeting in a building or at a location not normally open to the public? For example, could a public body hold a retreat at a gated resort community?

Only if the public body makes arrangements such that any citizen who wishes to attend the meeting is allowed into the private building or community without any unreasonable difficulty. The South Carolina Supreme Court has upheld having a meeting in such a location if appropriate arrangements to admit the public are made.[125]

---

123. *Id.* at 226.

124. *Id.* at 228 (no obligation under the open meetings law to modify the "first come, first served" nature of public access to public meetings in order to reserve seating for disabled persons).

125. Wiedemann v. Town of Hilton Head Island, 500 S.E.2d 783, 785 (S.C. 1998) (State law dictates that a balancing test is appropriate to determine whether such a meeting complies with the "minimum cost or delay.").

203.   Does the open meetings law prohibit boards from holding meetings outside their unit?

No. As long as proper notice is given of a meeting held outside the unit and the public is permitted to attend, the statute's requirements are satisfied. Local governing boards often hold retreats at locations outside their unit's boundaries.

204.   Aren't boards of county commissioners prohibited from holding meetings outside the county?

Yes, but this isn't a requirement of the open meetings law. This limitation is included in separate meeting requirements applicable only to boards of county commissioners. These meeting requirements are summarized in Question 234.

205.   The answer to Question 20 indicated that a conference telephone call among the members of a public body constitutes an official meeting. How can the public have access to such a meeting?

The law requires a public body that holds a meeting by electronic means to provide a location and means whereby the public may listen to the meeting. The notice of the meeting must specify the location.

206.   The necessary amplification equipment might be expensive. Can the cost be passed on to those who listen to the meeting?

Yes. The public body may charge up to $25 to each listener to defray the cost of the location and equipment.

207.   Does the open meetings law permit members of the public to record open meetings?

Yes. In fact it goes somewhat beyond that. First, it entitles any radio or television station to broadcast all or any part of the open session portion of a meeting. Second, it entitles any person—not just broadcasters—to photograph, film, tape-record, or otherwise reproduce the open session portion of any meeting.

208. May the public body regulate the people who broadcast or tape the meeting?

Yes. It may specify where the equipment is placed and how it is used and even, if the room becomes overly crowded, require that broadcasting and other equipment be pooled. However, a public body's regulations may not be so strict as to prevent the intended use of the equipment. The public body has no authority to restrict which portions of an open meeting may be recorded or photographed, and may not restrict the use of such recordings or photographs.

209. Some public bodies live stream their meetings and post the video on their websites. How long must the recordings of these meetings be retained?

Live streaming is not legally required. If these records are not being used as the official minutes, the unit can decide how long to keep them. See Question 192 regarding the use of recordings as minutes.

210. Some public bodies decide not to broadcast the entire meeting—for example, excluding the public comment period. Is that legal?

Yes. Since there is no obligation to broadcast it at all, the unit can determine what portions to include.

211. Can members of public bodies vote in secret?

No. The open meetings law prohibits secret ballots, and there are no exceptions to the prohibition.[126] But the law does permit written ballots if they are signed and made available for public inspection immediately after the meeting. The results of any voting by written ballot must also appear in the minutes and show how each member voted.

---

126. G.S. 143-318.13(b).

212. If the ballots must be signed, why are they used?

Sometimes a board will want to vote without each member knowing how the others have voted until all have voted. The signed ballot permits such a vote.

213. May a public body use secret ballots in a closed session?

Probably not. As already noted, the statute prohibits them. Therefore, even in a closed session, a public body may use written, but not secret, ballots.

214. Does the open meetings law prohibit one member of a public body from whispering to another during an open session of the public body?

No. But an attempt by the majority of the members of a public body to carry on a whispered conversation during a meeting probably would be held to violate the statute.

215. Is it illegal for members of public bodies to email or text during a meeting?

It depends on what they're saying and how many of them are doing it. If a majority of a public body is using electronic devices during a meeting to communicate simultaneously among themselves about the business of the public body, they could be violating the law, since the communication is not open to the public. In addition, if the texts or emails relate to public business, they would be public records.

216. May a board member participate in a meeting remotely by phone, video conference, or other means?

This raises the question of whether a member of a public body is legally required to be physically present at an official meeting. The answer depends on what type of public body is involved. The open meetings law definition of *official meeting* includes electronic meetings. But the law applies to all public bodies throughout the state, not just local government boards, and it does not address what types and formats of meetings public bodies can hold. The quorum and voting statutes for cities and counties refer to members being "present," but courts in other states have found that a person may be considered to be present when participating remotely.[127]

Until there is more specific guidance from the legislature or the courts, remote participation may create a risk if the remote participant casts a deciding vote or his or her presence is necessary to create a quorum. That is, since the law is unclear, a quorum that depends on the remote member is subject to later challenge, as is a deciding vote cast by that member. On the other hand, there is no legal risk if the remote member participates in a discussion (no vote being taken) or if a sufficient number of board members are physically present to constitute a quorum. It is up to the governing board, in any event, to decide whether and under what circumstances to allow remote participation. Local governments may also authorize remote participation for boards they create and appoint. Boards that wish to allow remote participation should establish policies governing when it will be allowed.[128]

217. If someone disrupts a meeting, can the public body ask the person to leave, or have him or her removed?

Yes. The statute provides that a person who "willfully interrupts, disturbs, or disrupts" an official meeting can be asked or directed to leave. If the person willfully refuses to leave after being directed

---

127. *See* Tuzeer v. Yim, LLC, 29 A.3d 1019, 1034 (Md. Ct. Spec. App. 2011) (citing Freedom Oil Co. v. Illinois Pollution Control Bd., 655 N.E.2d 1184, 1191 (Ill. App. Ct. 1995)), *cert. denied*, 35 A.3d 489 (Md. 2012) (phone participation by zoning board member did not violate open meetings law).

128. For a more detailed analysis of the legal aspects of remote participation, along with considerations for local policies, see Frayda S. Bluestein, "Remote Participation in Local Government Board Meetings," *Local Government Law Bulletin* 133 (School of Government, August 2013), http://sogpubs.unc.edu/electronicversions/pdfs/lglb133.pdf.

to do so by the presiding officer, that person is guilty of a Class 2 misdemeanor.[129]

218. Does this provision apply to board members as well as to the public?

The statute does not distinguish between the public and board members, and so it appears to apply to board members as well. Courts have upheld the actions of presiding officers who direct disruptive members of the public body to leave the meeting.[130]

Remedies

219. Is a meeting that violates the open meetings law "illegal" and, if so, are the actions taken, if any, automatically void?

Nothing automatically happens to invalidate a meeting when a violation of the open meetings law occurs. If a violation becomes apparent, it is wise for the public body to consider whether a new meeting should be convened to ratify any actions taken in the unlawful meeting. Someone must initiate a lawsuit, however, for any legal consequence to result.

220. Well, what if someone files a lawsuit? What kinds of sanctions can a court impose?

The law provides three separate remedies. The first and most simple is a declaratory judgment, in which a court simply finds that a violation has occurred. The court assumes that the public body will follow the law in the future, and therefore there will be no

---

129. G.S 143-318.17

130. *See* King v. Jefferies, 402 F. Supp. 2d 624 (M.D.N.C. 2005) (board member removed from closed session after refusing to refrain from recording the meeting); Wysinger v. City of Benton Harbor, 968 F. Supp. 349 (W.D. Mich. 1997) (rejecting a First Amendment challenge to a mayor's action ejecting a city commissioner from a meeting because the commissioner was disruptive).

other effects from the judgment. Second, any person may also seek an injunction against threatened, past, or continuing violations; in this case the court orders the public body to avoid similar violations in the future. Third, and perhaps most severe, a person may seek a court order invalidating any action taken, considered, discussed, or deliberated in violation of the act.

221. The possibility that an action might be declared invalid certainly is a potentially severe remedy. If a court finds a violation has occurred and the plaintiff asks for invalidation, is the court required to hold the action invalid?

No. Trial judges may or may not hold the action invalid. That decision is within their discretion.

222. What factors will the judge consider in deciding whether to invalidate an action?

The statute directs the judge to consider at least the following factors.

- How much did the violation affect the substance of the challenged action?
- How much did the violation impair public access to the meeting or proceedings involved?
- How much did the violation prevent public knowledge or understanding of the matter at issue?
- Was the violation an isolated event or was it part of a continuing pattern of violations?
- Have others relied on the challenged action, and what would be the effect on them of declaring it invalid?
- Did the public body violate the law in bad faith, with the intention of subverting the statutory policy?

223. Are there any other factors, not listed in the statute, that a trial court might consider in deciding whether to invalidate an action?

One court, in another state, noted that the plaintiffs had never pointed out to the public body that it had violated the law, and thus the public body had never had a chance to remedy the violation on its own. Therefore the court refused to invalidate the action. This case raises the basic question of whether a violation can be cured or the offending action ratified.[131]

224. Does North Carolina law permit curing a violation or ratifying an action affected by a violation?

The law says nothing at all about cures or ratifications, and the experience from other states with a comparable statutory silence is mixed. A growing majority of courts in such states, however, allow curing the violation or ratifying (or retaking) the action. Therefore, if a court feels that the cure or ratification overcomes the negative factors that might otherwise have caused the court to invalidate the action, there is a good chance the cure or ratification will be accepted. If the negative factors are not overcome, however, the action will be invalidated despite the attempt at cure or ratification. The courts seem more willing to accept an attempted ratification if the ratification follows a full public reconsideration and debate of the matter by the public body. (Of course, even if the court has invalidated an action, the public body can once more begin the process leading to the action.)

For example, a number of courts have refused to invalidate actions affected by improper notice of a meeting when the public body has given proper notice of a later meeting and redone the proceedings of the first meeting. On the other hand, courts have also invalidated actions taken at a fully public meeting when violations that occurred at earlier stages may have affected the

---

131. *See* Rehabilitation Hosp. Servs. Corp. v. Delta Hills Health Sys. Agency, Inc., 687 S.W.2d 840 (Ark. 1985).

substance of the action or kept the public from a crucial stage in the decision-making process.[132]

225. What kinds of actions are likely to be held invalid?

Courts in other states have held a wide variety of actions invalid because of a violation of an open meetings law. Among the sorts of actions that have been commonly challenged are rezonings and other land use decisions, annexations, contracts, property sales, rate-setting, and personnel actions. In a number of cases, persons in litigation with the public body have sought to invalidate various steps taken by the body in the litigation process, such as the decision to bring the lawsuit or to file an appeal. If an action is controversial and opponents decide to challenge the action in court, a public body should expect those opponents to look for an open meetings violation as one ground on which to invalidate the action.

---

132. The cases mentioned in the text in which a court refused to invalidate an action because it had been cured include *Cooper v. Arizona Western College District Governing Board*, 610 P.2d 465 (Ariz. Ct. App. 1980); *Board of Education v. Sikorski*, 574 N.E.2d 736 (Ill. App. Ct. 1991); *Allen v. Board of Selectmen*, 792 N.E.2d 1000 (Mass. App. Ct. 2003); *Pokorny v. City of Schuyler*, 275 N.W.2d 281 (Neb. 1979); *Board of Education v. Brown*, 558 A.2d 520 (N.J. Super. Ct. App. Div. 1989); *Kleinberg v. Board of Education*, 751 P.2d 722 (N.M. Ct. App. 1988); *Multimedia, Inc. v. Greenville Airport Commission*, 339 S.E.2d 884 (S.C. Ct. App. 1986); *Neese v. Paris Special School District*, 813 S.W.2d 432 (Tenn. Ct. App. 1990); and *Ward v. Richfield City*, 798 P.2d 757 (Utah 1990). The cases in which the court has invalidated the action, even though it was taken at an open meeting, are *Littleton Education Association v. Arapahoe County School District*, 553 P.2d 793 (Colo. 1976); *Biglow v. Howze*, 291 So. 2d 645 (Fla. Dist. Ct. App. 1974); and *Peters v. Bowman Public School District Number 1*, 231 N.W.2d 817 (N.D. 1975). Cases in which the court required a public reconsideration of the issue include *Webster County Board of Education v. Franklin*, 392 S.W.3d 431, 436 (Ky. Ct. App. 2013), and *Van Alstyne v. Housing Authority of the City of Pueblo, Colorado*, 985 P.2d 97 (Colo. Ct. App. 1999) (ratification refused because there was no full reconsideration by the public body).

226. Invalidating an action could be extremely disruptive. Is there any kind of statute of limitations on lawsuits to invalidate actions under the open meetings law?

Yes, and it's quite short. If the action involves a bond order or bond referendum, the 30-day statute of limitations set out in G.S. 159-59 or G.S. 159-62 applies. For any other action, the plaintiff must bring the lawsuit within 45 days after the action appears in the minutes or, if the action is not recorded in the minutes, within 45 days of the time the plaintiff knew or should have known of the action.[133]

227. Let's return for a minute to the second remedy, the injunction. What's the effect of such a court order?

An injunction prohibits the public body from violating the statute in the future in the same way it violated that law in the past. If an injunction is awarded and then violated (that is, if the public body repeats the prohibited violation), then its members are in contempt of court and can be fined.

228. Is it possible that a public body might have to pay the attorneys' fees of someone who claims that the public body violated the open meetings law?

Definitely. On the other hand, it's possible that the plaintiff might end up paying the public body's attorneys' fees. If a lawsuit is brought under the open meetings law, regardless of the remedy the plaintiff seeks, the trial court is allowed by statute to identify the prevailing party or parties in the lawsuit. It then may (but need

---

133. *See* Sandi's II v. Assumption Parish Police Jury, 837 So. 2d 124 (La. Ct. App. 2002) (implementing a 60-day statute of limitations); Coulter v. City of Newton, 100 N.C. App. 523 (1990) (interpreting when plaintiffs first knew of an action allegedly in violation of the law); Bradford Area Educ. Ass'n v. Bradford Area Sch. Dist., 572 A.2d 1314 (Pa. Commw. Ct. 1990) (interpreting a comparable statutory provision).

not) order the other side to pay the reasonable attorneys' fees of the prevailing party. Thus, if the plaintiff proves that a violation has occurred, the public body might have to pay the plaintiff's attorneys' fees. But if no violation is proved, the plaintiff might have to pay the public body's attorneys' fees, although this is likely only if the action is frivolous.

229. Normally if attorneys' fees are required to be paid, the government itself will pay them. Might the board members who committed the violation ever have to pay the attorneys' fees for the other side?

Yes. The statute allows the judge to require the plaintiffs' attorneys' fees to be paid personally by the board members if the court finds the violation was knowingly or intentionally committed. If the board members acted upon the advice of an attorney, however, they cannot be made to pay the fees.

Related Public Meeting Topics

This section provides answers to questions about meetings and related topics that involve legal requirements outside of the open meetings law.

Additional Notice and Meetings Requirements for City and County Governing Boards

230. The open meetings law notice requirements are directed to the general public and the media. What are the notice requirements directed to members of city and county governing boards?

G.S. Chapters 160A (for cities) and 153A (for counties) establish meeting requirements that are separate from the open meetings law. Both sets of requirements must be met. There are no such provisions in Chapter 115C for local school boards. These provisions establish a requirement for regular meetings, and they specify how and when meetings may be called and what type of notice must be given to the members of the board.

231. What are the requirements for holding regular meetings?

For counties, G.S. 153A-40 directs boards of county commissioners to hold at least one meeting each month, although they may meet more often if necessary. The statute requires the board to set the schedule of regular meetings by resolution, and, at least 10 days before the first meeting, post it on the courthouse bulletin board and publish a summary of it. Many boards hold two regular meetings each month. The board may select any day of the month and any public place within the county for its regular meetings, but unless it selects some other time or place by formal resolution, the law requires the board to meet on the first Monday of the month at the courthouse. There is no statutory remedy or sanction for a county's failure to hold a meeting in a particular month.

For cities, G.S. 160A-71 directs each city's governing board to fix the time and the place of its regular meetings. If the board fails to act, the statute provides that meetings shall be held on the first Monday of each month at 10:00 a.m. Cities are not required to hold a meeting every month.

232. What types of special meetings are allowed and what are the notice requirements for these types of meetings?

Although both county commissioners and city councils may hold special meetings, the statutes under which they may do so are somewhat different. The statutes that apply to city and county governing bodies define a *special meeting* as any meeting other than a regular meeting. These requirements must be met *in addition to* the notice requirements in the open meetings law.

A special meeting of the county board of commissioners may be called by the chair or by a majority of the other board members.

It must be called by written notice stating the time, place, and subjects to be considered. This notice must be posted on the courthouse bulletin board and delivered to each board member at least 48 hours before the meeting. Unless all members attend or sign a written waiver, only business related to the subjects stated in the notice may be transacted at a special meeting. However, expanding the subjects to be addressed in a special meeting, even if allowed under this statute, may violate the open meetings law.[134]

A special meeting of the city council may be called in either of two ways. First, if a board is convened in a regular meeting or a duly called special meeting, it may schedule a special meeting. Second, the mayor, the mayor pro tempore, or any two members of the board may call such a meeting. They may do so by preparing and signing a written notice of the meeting—setting out the time, place, and the subjects to be considered—and having this notice delivered to each board member (or to the member's home). The same restriction on subjects that applies to counties applies to cities. Only matters stated in the notice may be taken up in the special meeting unless all members attend or sign a written waiver. The notice must be delivered to members at least 6 hours before the meeting, but as noted earlier, the open meetings law requires 48 hours' *public* notice of a special meeting. Thus, except in an emergency, the board cannot legally meet within less than 48 hours despite the shorter notice period for members.

233. Are there special rules for emergency meetings under these statutes?

For counties, G.S. 153A-40 provides that the notice to board members is not required for a special meeting called to deal with an emergency, but it does require that the person or persons calling the meeting take reasonable actions to inform the other members and the public of the meeting.

---

134. See Question 67.

The city statutes do not specifically address emergency meetings. Thus, the 6-hour notice for special meetings applies to these types of meetings. Even though there is no minimum time for public notice of emergency meetings under the open meetings law, the 6-hour board member notice requirement will usually limit a city's ability to hold a meeting with less than 6 hours' notice. If, however, an emergency meeting is set during a regular or duly called special meeting, the 6-hour notice requirement does not apply.

234. What are the limitations on meeting places?

As noted in Question 196, meeting locations must reasonably accommodate the public. In addition to this general requirement, there is a specific locational limitation for county boards of commissioners. Their meetings must be held within the county. G.S. 153A-40 permits out-of-county meetings in only four specific instances:

- In connection with a joint meeting of two or more public bodies, as long as the meeting is within the boundaries of the political subdivision represented by the members of one of the participating bodies
- In connection with a retreat, forum, or similar gathering held solely to provide the county commissioners with information relating to the performance of their public duties (no vote may be taken during this type of meeting)
- In connection with a meeting between the board and its local legislative delegation while the General Assembly is in session, as long as no votes are taken except concerning matters directly relating to proposed or pending legislation
- While the commissioners are attending a convention, association meeting, or similar gathering, if the meeting is held solely to discuss or deliberate on the board's position concerning convention resolutions, association officer elections, and similar issues that are not legally binding

There are no comparable statutory restrictions on the location of city council meetings.

Requirements for Public Hearings and Public Comment Periods

235. When are public hearings required?

Although it might be assumed that a public hearing is required whenever an ordinance is adopted or amended, that's not the case. No single general law stipulates when public hearings must be held; instead, a public hearing is required only when a specific statute calls for it. One familiar example is the statute that requires public hearings for zoning map and text amendments. And, of course, there must be a hearing before the adoption of the annual budget ordinance. But most types of ordinances and other actions do not require public hearings. Many boards voluntarily hold public hearings, especially about controversial proposals, even when the law does not require them. A compilation of required public hearings for cities and counties (as of the date of this publication) is set out in Appendix 2 of this book.

236. How much and what type of notice must be given for a public hearing?

There is no general answer to this question. The type and timing of notice required are typically set out in the statute that requires the public hearing. In cases where the statute omits this information, a good practice is to allow at least 10 days' notice, and to provide notice by publication in outlets and venues accessible to members of the public who may be interested in the matter.

237. Must a quorum be present for a public hearing?

Generally, yes, especially if the matter that is the subject of the hearing will be decided by a public body, or if the statute specifically requires that a particular public body must hold the hearing. In these cases the public hearing must occur at a legally convened meeting of the public body. Although no North Carolina case specifically addresses this point, a case from Georgia notes that a quorum is necessary for a public hearing because it is part of the board's official business. Indeed, "conducting hearings" is one of the activities of a public body that constitutes an official meeting under the open meetings law. In addition, parallel statutes for cities and counties provide that if a quorum is not present for a public hearing, the hearing must be continued until the next regular meeting without further advertisement.[135] If the public hearing is not statutorily required, however, the members present may choose to allow it to go forward without a quorum being present, and there is no legal consequence. Also, in some cases a hearing occurs before an individual rather than a public body, but those types of hearings are typically of a different sort, as described in the next Question.

238. What are "quasi-judicial" hearings and when are they required?

Quasi-judicial hearings are required when a person has a type of property interest that triggers due process requirements under the state and federal constitutions. Typically standards for these proceedings are set in a statute, ordinance, or case law, and the governmental body's role is as a judge, making an objective decision by applying the facts to the law.[136] So this type of hearing is completely different from a general public hearing. It is not a forum for public comment, but is more like a trial. Participation is limited to people with standing, and their comments must be relevant and not just based on opinion. Examples include hearings on variances, special or conditional use permits, and appeals from administrative decisions on matters such as minimum housing requirements, as well as appeals about employment actions.

---

135. G.S. 160A-81 (cities); G.S. 153A-52 (counties).

136. *See* Humble Oil & Refining Co. v. Bd. of Aldermen, 284 N.C. 458, 468 (1974).

239. When and why are public comment periods required?

As noted earlier, the open meetings law allows the public to attend meetings, but they have no right to speak. Many local governments provide time on their regular agendas for public comment, but until 2005, there was no legal requirement to do so. Legislation enacted that year requires city, county, and school boards to provide a period of time for public comment at a regular meeting at least once per month.[137] The public comment period is not required if the board does not have a regular meeting in a particular month.

240. May the local government adopt rules governing the conduct of public hearings and comment periods?

Yes. State law provides limited authority for cities and counties to regulate the conduct of public hearings and comment periods.[138] For cities, public hearings may be held at any place within the city or within the county in which the city is located; for counties, at any place within the county. The statutes also allow the governing board to adopt "reasonable rules governing the conduct of public hearings," including rules (1) fixing the maximum time allotted to each speaker, (2) providing for the designation of spokesmen for groups of persons supporting or opposing the same positions, (3) providing for the selection of delegates from groups of persons supporting or opposing the same positions when the number of persons wishing to attend the hearing exceeds the capacity of the hall, and (4) providing for the maintenance of order and decorum in the conduct of the hearing. The same rules provision applies to public comment periods.

---

137. G.S. 153A-52.1 (counties); G.S. 160A-81.1 (cities); G.S. 115C-51 (schools).

138. G.S. 160A-81 (cities); G.S. 153A-52 (counties).

241. May a local board adopt rules about who can speak at public hearings or public comment periods and what topics they may address? Could the local government, for example, allow only residents or property owners from the jurisdiction to speak?

Except for the provisions discussed in the previous Question, there is no specific authority to restrict who can speak or what topics they may address. There is probably implicit authority to restrict comments to the subject of the public hearing. At public comment periods, the local government may have the ability to limit comments to matters that relate in some way to the jurisdiction and authority of the local government. Other types of restrictions are probably not allowed. Public hearings and comment periods are a type of designated forum for free speech.[139] The statutes authorize what amount to content-neutral time, place, and manner limitations.[140] Residency or viewpoint-based restrictions are not authorized and would very likely be invalidated if challenged in court.

242. Do these same rules apply to a quasi-judicial hearing, such as a hearing on a conditional use permit or a disciplinary hearing regarding a personnel matter?

No. As noted in Question 238, quasi-judicial hearings are quite different from public hearings. These hearings have a distinct legal purpose, which is to allow parties with specifically identifiable interests or expertise regarding the matter to present evidence, and to allow affected parties to hear and cross-examine

---

139. *See* Surita v. Hyde, 665 F.3d 860, 869 (7th Cir. 2011); Galena v. Leone, 638 F.3d 186, 198–99 (3d Cir. 2011); Steinburg v. Chesterfield Cty. Planning Comm'n, 527 F.3d 377, 384–86 (4th Cir. 2008); Eichenlaub v. Twp. of Ind., 385 F.3d 274, 280–81 (3d Cir. 2004); Rowe v. City of Cocoa, Fla., 358 F.3d 900, 902 (11th Cir. 2004).

140. *See Galena*, 638 F.3d at 198 (citing Pleasant Grove City v. Summum, 555 U.S. 460, 470 (2009)).

the speakers. Participation in these types of hearings is limited to those with standing or expertise, and topics must be relevant to the matter at hand.

Appendix 1

Quick-Reference Guide to Closed Sessions

General Requirements for Closed Sessions

- Comply with notice requirements for the meeting, even if the entire meeting will consist of a closed session.
- Begin the meeting in open session.
- Adopt a motion to go into closed session.
- State in the motion the authorized purpose(s) for the closed session. There is no legal requirement to include the statutory citation; a description of the provision that authorizes the closed session is sufficient.
- In two special cases, include additional information in the motion. (See italicized information in the list on the following page.)
- Ensure that everyone attending the closed session is legally authorized to be present. The public body may, in its discretion, decide who may attend a closed session, except in three circumstances listed on the next page.
- Return to open session after completing the closed session.
- Create minutes and a general account of the closed session.
- Determine whether minutes and the general account may be withheld from the public to avoid frustrating the purpose of the closed session.

Requirements for Specific Types of Closed Sessions

To protect confidential or privileged information (G.S. 143-318.11(a)(1))

- *Motion must state the name or citation of the law that renders the information confidential or privileged.*
- Attendance is limited to people who legally have access to the confidential or privileged information.

To consult with an attorney to protect the attorney–client privilege (G.S. 143-318.11(a)(3))

- *For discussion of existing litigation, the motion must identify the parties to the lawsuit.*
- The attorney must participate in the meeting to provide legal consultation with the public body.
- The public body may instruct the attorney about pending matters, including approving a settlement.
- Settlements approved in closed session must be reported to the public body in open session within a reasonable time after the settlement is concluded.
- Attendance is limited to people who are within the attorney–client privilege.

To discuss the location or expansion of industries or other businesses in the area served by the public body (G.S. 143-381.11(a)(4))

- Approval of specific economic development incentives, contracts, or expenditures must occur in open session.
- Must involve specific prospects, not general policies or speculative projects.

To establish the public body's negotiating position for acquisition of real property or employment contracts or instruct staff or agents about the negotiation (G.S. 143-381.11(a)(5))

- Cannot be used to discuss the *sale* of property by the public body, unless it is an exchange in which the unit acquires real property.
- Discussion of *which* property to acquire is not allowed in closed session.
- The public body, *upon request*, must disclose, before it enters the closed session, (1) the property's current owner, (2) the property's location, and (3) the purposes for which the public body intends use the property.
- The public body may agree on a final position as an instruction to a staff member or agent.

To address personnel matters (G.S. 143-381.11(a)(6))

- Discussion must be about one or more individual employees and cannot involve general policy issues.
- Cannot be used to discuss independent contractors, except possibly the unit's contracted attorney.
- Cannot be used to discuss members of the public body itself or any other public body, including applicants for appointment to any public body.
- Session can be used to hear or investigate a complaint, charge, or grievance by or against an individual public officer or employee.
- Final action to make an appointment, discharge, or removal must be made in open session.
- If the discussion involves confidential information or records (which it often does), attendance is limited to those who have legal access to the confidential information or records.

Appendix 2

Compilation of Statutorily Required Public Hearings for Cities and Counties

The open meetings law applies to meetings but does not set out requirements for public hearings. A public hearing may be part of a meeting, but in some cases, separate notice and other procedural requirements will apply to the public hearing itself. A recurrent question is: When *must* a city council or board of county commissioners hold a public hearing? The following compilation lists requirements for public hearings for cities and counties. For more information about requirements for public hearings, see Questions 235–242.

Measure	G.S. County Cite	G.S. City Cite
Adopting regulatory ordinances		
Development ordinances	153A-323	160A-364
Sunday closing ordinances		160A-191
Government structure		
Form of government		160A-102
Fire district expansion	69-25.11	
Sanitary district creation	130A-48	
City parking authority creation		160A-552
County commissioners exercising control of commissions, boards, and agencies	153A-77(a)	

(continued)

Measure	G.S. County Cite	G.S. City Cite
Service district matters		
Establishing districts	153A-302	160A-537
Petition to establish district		160A-537(a1), (c)
Expanding districts	153A-303	160A-538
Deleting territory		160A-538.1
Petition to exclude territory		160A-538.1(a1)
Consolidating districts	153A-304	160A-539
Adjusting boundaries	153A-304.3	
Abolishing districts	153A-306	160A-541
Contracting with private agencies (certain districts)		160A-536(d1)(3)
Establishing some fire districts	153A-309.2	
Establishing industrial fire districts	153A-309.3	
Establishing some EMS districts	153A-310	
Establishing research/production districts	153A-312	
Expanding research/production districts	153A-314	
Deleting territory from research/production districts	153A-314.1	
Abolishing research/production districts	153A-316	
Establishing economic development/ training districts	153A-317.12	
Expanding economic development/training districts	153A-317.14	
Abolishing economic development/training districts	153A-317.16	
Municipal annexation		
Voluntary contiguous		160A-31
Voluntary satellite		160A-58.2
Involuntary		160A-58.55
Annexation agreements		160A-58.24

(continued)

Measure	G.S. County Cite	G.S. City Cite
Financial matters		
Annual budget ordinance	159-12	159-12
General obligation bonds	159-57	159-57
Installment financings	160A-20	160A-20
Acquiring college property	153A-158.2	
Levy of occupancy taxes	153A-155	160A-215
Establishing stormwater fees	153A-277	160A-314
Special assessments		
Preliminary resolution	153A-192	160A-225
Preliminary assessment roll	153A-195	160A-228
Development fees (new or increased)	153A-102.1(b)	160A-4.1(b)
Streets and roads		
Closing streets and roads	153A-241	160A-299
Naming roads, assigning numbers	153A-239.1	
Permitting bridges	153A-243	
Transportation corridor map	136-44.50	136-44.50
Transportation plan		136-66.2
Miscellaneous		
Economic development incentives	158-7.1	158-7.1
Solid waste management plans	130A-309.09A	130A-309.09A
Coastal area land use plans	113-110(e)	113-110(e)
Landfill site selection	153A-136(c)	160A-325(a)
Ambulance service ordinances	153A-250	153A-250
Location of ABC stores		18B-801
Minority business participation goals	143-128.2	143-128.2

Appendix 3

Text of the Open Meetings Statute

Article 33C.

Meetings of Public Bodies.

§ 143-318.9. Public policy.

Whereas the public bodies that administer the legislative, policy-making, quasi-judicial, administrative, and advisory functions of North Carolina and its political subdivisions exist solely to conduct the people's business, it is the public policy of North Carolina that the hearings, deliberations, and actions of these bodies be conducted openly.

§ 143-318.10. All official meetings of public bodies open to the public.

(a) Except as provided in G.S. 143-318.11, 143-318.14A, and 143-318.18, each official meeting of a public body shall be open to the public, and any person is entitled to attend such a meeting.

(b) As used in this Article, "public body" means any elected or appointed authority, board, commission, committee, council, or other body of the State, or of one or more counties, cities, school administrative units, constituent institutions of The University of North Carolina, or other political subdivisions or public corporations in the State that (i) is composed of two or more members and (ii) exercises or is authorized to exercise a legislative, policy-making, quasi-judicial, administrative, or advisory function. In addition, "public body" means the governing board of a "public hospital" as defined in G.S. 159-39 and the governing board of any nonprofit corporation to which a hospital facility has been sold or conveyed pursuant to G.S. 131E-8, any subsidiary of such nonprofit corporation, and any nonprofit corporation owning the corporation to which the hospital facility has been sold or conveyed.

(c) "Public body" does not include (i) a meeting solely among the professional staff of a public body, or (ii) the medical staff of a public hospital or the medical staff of a hospital that has been sold or conveyed pursuant to G.S. 131E-8.

(d) "Official meeting" means a meeting, assembly, or gathering together at any time or place or the simultaneous communication by conference telephone or other electronic means of a majority of the members of a public body for the purpose of conducting hearings, participating in deliberations, or voting upon or otherwise transacting the public business within the jurisdiction, real or apparent, of the public body. However, a social meeting or other informal assembly or gathering together of the members of a public body does not constitute an official meeting unless called or held to evade the spirit and purposes of this Article.

(e) Every public body shall keep full and accurate minutes of all official meetings, including any closed sessions held pursuant to G.S. 143-318.11. Such minutes may be in written form or, at the option of the public body, may be in the form of sound or video and sound recordings. When a public body meets in closed session, it shall keep a general account of the closed session so that a person not in attendance would have a reasonable understanding of what transpired. Such accounts may be a written narrative, or video or audio recordings. Such minutes and accounts shall be public records within the meaning of the Public Records Law, G.S. 132-1 et seq.; provided, however, that minutes or an account of a closed session conducted in compliance with G.S. 143-318.11 may be withheld from public inspection so long as public inspection would frustrate the purpose of a closed session.

§ 143-318.11. Closed sessions.

(a) Permitted Purposes.—It is the policy of this State that closed sessions shall be held only when required to permit a public body to act in the public interest as permitted in this section. A public body may hold a closed session and exclude the public only when a closed session is required:

(1) To prevent the disclosure of information that is privileged or confidential pursuant to the law of this State or of the United States, or not considered a public record within the meaning of Chapter 132 of the General Statutes.

(2) To prevent the premature disclosure of an honorary degree, scholarship, prize, or similar award.

(3) To consult with an attorney employed or retained by the public body in order to preserve the attorney-client privilege between the attorney and the public body, which privilege is hereby acknowledged. General policy matters may not be discussed in a closed session and nothing herein shall be construed to permit a public body to close a meeting that otherwise would be open merely because an attorney employed or retained by the public body is a participant. The public body may consider and give instructions to an attorney concerning the handling or settlement of a claim, judicial action, mediation, arbitration, or administrative procedure. If the public body has approved or considered a settlement, other than a malpractice settlement by or on behalf of a hospital, in closed session, the terms of that settlement shall be reported to the public body and entered into its

minutes as soon as possible within a reasonable time after the settlement is concluded.

(4) To discuss matters relating to the location or expansion of industries or other businesses in the area served by the public body, including agreement on a tentative list of economic development incentives that may be offered by the public body in negotiations, or to discuss matters relating to military installation closure or realignment. Any action approving the signing of an economic development contract or commitment, or the action authorizing the payment of economic development expenditures, shall be taken in an open session.

(5) To establish, or to instruct the public body's staff or negotiating agents concerning the position to be taken by or on behalf of the public body in negotiating (i) the price and other material terms of a contract or proposed contract for the acquisition of real property by purchase, option, exchange, or lease; or (ii) the amount of compensation and other material terms of an employment contract or proposed employment contract.

(6) To consider the qualifications, competence, performance, character, fitness, conditions of appointment, or conditions of initial employment of an individual public officer or employee or prospective public officer or employee; or to hear or investigate a complaint, charge, or grievance by or against an individual public officer or employee. General personnel policy issues may not be considered in a closed session. A public body may not consider the qualifications, competence, performance, character, fitness, appointment, or removal of a member of the public body or another body and may not consider or fill a vacancy among its own membership except in an

open meeting. Final action making an appointment or discharge or removal by a public body having final authority for the appointment or discharge or removal shall be taken in an open meeting.

(7)   To plan, conduct, or hear reports concerning investigations of alleged criminal misconduct.

(8)   To formulate plans by a local board of education relating to emergency response to incidents of school violence or to formulate and adopt the school safety components of school improvement plans by a local board of education or a school improvement team.

(9)   To discuss and take action regarding plans to protect public safety as it relates to existing or potential terrorist activity and to receive briefings by staff members, legal counsel, or law enforcement or emergency service officials concerning actions taken or to be taken to respond to such activity.

(10) To view a recording released pursuant to G.S. 132-1.4A.

(b) Repealed by Laws 1991, c. 694, § 4.

(c) Calling a Closed Session.—A public body may hold a closed session only upon a motion duly made and adopted at an open meeting. Every motion to close a meeting shall cite one or more of the permissible purposes listed in subsection (a) of this section. A motion based on subdivision (a)(1) of this section shall also state the name or citation of the law that renders the information to be discussed privileged or confidential. A motion based on subdivision (a)(3) of this section shall identify the parties in each existing lawsuit concerning which the public body expects to receive advice during the closed session.

(d) Repealed by Laws 1993, c. 570, § 2, eff. Oct. 1, 1994.

§ 143-318.12. Public notice of official meetings.

(a) If a public body has established, by ordinance, resolution, or otherwise, a schedule of regular meetings, it shall cause a current copy of that schedule, showing the time and place of regular meetings, to be kept on file as follows:

    (1)   For public bodies that are part of State government, with the Secretary of State;

    (2)   For the governing board and each other public body that is part of a county government, with the clerk to the board of county commissioners;

    (3)   For the governing board and each other public body that is part of a city government, with the city clerk;

    (4)   For each other public body, with its clerk or secretary, or, if the public body does not have a clerk or secretary, with the clerk to the board of county commissioners in the county in which the public body normally holds its meetings.

If a public body changes its schedule of regular meetings, it shall cause the revised schedule to be filed as provided in subdivisions (1) through (4) of this subsection at least seven calendar days before the day of the first meeting held pursuant to the revised schedule.

(b) If a public body holds an official meeting at any time or place other than a time or place shown on the schedule filed pursuant to subsection (a) of this section, it shall give public notice of the time and place of that meeting as provided in this subsection.

    (1)   If a public body recesses a regular, special, or emergency meeting held pursuant to public notice given in compliance with this subsection, and the time and place at which the meeting is to be continued is announced in open session, no further notice shall be required.

    (2)   For any other meeting, except an emergency meeting, the public body shall cause written notice of

the meeting stating its purpose (i) to be posted on the principal bulletin board of the public body or, if the public body has no such bulletin board, at the door of its usual meeting room, and (ii) to be mailed, e-mailed, or delivered to each newspaper, wire service, radio station, and television station that has filed a written request for notice with the clerk or secretary of the public body or with some other person designated by the public body. The public body shall also cause notice to be mailed, e-mailed, or delivered to any person, in addition to the representatives of the media listed above, who has filed a written request with the clerk, secretary, or other person designated by the public body. This notice shall be posted and mailed, e-mailed, or delivered at least 48 hours before the time of the meeting. The notice required to be posted on the principal bulletin board or at the door of its usual meeting room shall be posted on the door of the building or on the building in an area accessible to the public if the building containing the principal bulletin board or usual meeting room is closed to the public continuously for 48 hours before the time of the meeting. The public body may require each newspaper, wire service, radio station, and television station submitting a written request for notice to renew the request annually. The public body shall charge a fee to persons other than the media, who request notice, of ten dollars ($10.00) per calendar year, and may require them to renew their requests quarterly. No fee shall be charged for notices sent by e-mail.

(3)   For an emergency meeting, the public body shall cause notice of the meeting to be given to each local newspaper, local wire service, local radio station, and local television station that has filed a written

request, which includes the newspaper's, wire service's, or station's telephone number, for emergency notice with the clerk or secretary of the public body or with some other person designated by the public body. This notice shall be given either by e-mail, by telephone, or by the same method used to notify the members of the public body and shall be given immediately after notice has been given to those members. This notice shall be given at the expense of the party notified. Only business connected with the emergency may be considered at a meeting to which notice is given pursuant to this paragraph.

(c) Repealed by S.L. 1991-694, § 6.

(d) If a public body has a Web site and has established a schedule of regular meetings, the public body shall post the schedule of regular meetings to the Web site.

(e) If a public body has a Web site that one or more of its employees maintains, the public body shall post notice of any meeting held under subdivisions (b)(1) and (b)(2) of this section prior to the scheduled time of that meeting.

(f) For purposes of this section, an "emergency meeting" is one called because of generally unexpected circumstances that require immediate consideration by the public body.

§ 143-318.13. Electronic meetings; written ballots; acting by reference.

(a) Electronic Meetings.—If a public body holds an official meeting by use of conference telephone or other electronic means, it shall provide a location and means whereby members of the public may listen to the meeting and the notice of the meeting required by this Article shall specify that location. A fee of up to twenty-five dollars ($25.00) may be charged each such listener to defray in part the cost of providing the necessary location and equipment.

(b) Written Ballots.—Except as provided in this subsection or by joint resolution of the General Assembly, a public body may not vote by secret or written ballot. If a public body decides to vote by written ballot, each member of the body so voting shall sign his or her ballot; and the minutes of the public body shall show the vote of each member voting. The ballots shall be available for public inspection in the office of the clerk or secretary to the public body immediately following the meeting at which the vote took place and until the minutes of that meeting are approved, at which time the ballots may be destroyed.

(c) Acting by Reference.—The members of a public body shall not deliberate, vote, or otherwise take action upon any matter by reference to a letter, number or other designation, or other secret device or method, with the intention of making it impossible for persons attending a meeting of the public body to understand what is being deliberated, voted, or acted upon. However, this subsection does not prohibit a public body from deliberating, voting, or otherwise taking action by reference to an agenda, if copies of the agenda, sufficiently worded to enable the public to understand what is being deliberated, voted, or acted upon, are available for public inspection at the meeting.

§ 143-318.14. Broadcasting or recording meetings.

(a) Except as herein below provided, any radio or television station is entitled to broadcast all or any part of a meeting required to be open. Any person may photograph, film, tape-record, or otherwise reproduce any part of a meeting required to be open.

(b) A public body may regulate the placement and use of equipment necessary for broadcasting, photographing, filming, or recording a meeting, so as to prevent undue interference with the meeting. However, the public body must allow such equipment to be placed within the meeting room in such a way as to permit its intended use, and the ordinary use of such equipment shall not be declared to constitute undue interference; provided, however, that if the public body, in good faith, should determine that the size of the meeting room is such that all the members of the public body, members of the public present, and the equipment and personnel necessary for broadcasting, photographing, filming, and tape-recording the meeting cannot be accommodated in the meeting room without unduly interfering with the meeting and an adequate alternative meeting room is not readily available, then the public body, acting in good faith and consistent with the purposes of this Article, may require the pooling of such equipment and the personnel operating it; and provided further, if the news media, in order to facilitate news coverage, request an alternate site for the meeting, and the public body grants the request, then the news media making such request shall pay any costs incurred by the public body in securing an alternate meeting site.

§ 143-318.14A. Legislative commissions, committees, and standing subcommittees.

(a) Except as provided in subsection (e) below, all official meetings of commissions, committees, and standing subcommittees of the General Assembly (including, without limitation, joint committees and study committees), shall be held in open session. For the purpose of this section, the following also shall be considered to be "commissions, committees, and standing subcommittees of the General Assembly":

(1)　The Legislative Research Commission;

(2)　The Legislative Services Commission;

(3)　Repealed by S.L. 2006-203, § 93, eff. July 1, 2007.

(4)　Repealed by S.L. 2011-291, § 2.50, eff. June 24, 2011.

(5)　The Joint Legislative Commission on Governmental Operations;

(6)　The Joint Legislative Commission [Committee] on Local Government;

(7)　Repealed by S.L. 1997-443, §. 12.30, eff. Aug. 28, 1997.

(8)　Repealed by S.L. 2011-291, § 2.50, eff. June 24, 2011.

(9)　The Environmental Review Commission;

(10) The Joint Legislative Transportation Oversight Committee;

(11) The Joint Legislative Education Oversight Committee;

(12) Repealed by S.L. 2011-291, § 2.50, eff. June 24, 2011; S.L. 2011-266, § 1.28(b), eff. July 1, 2011.

(13) The Commission on Children with Special Needs;

(14) Repealed by S.L. 2011-291, § 2.50, eff. June 24, 2011.

(15) The Agriculture and Forestry Awareness Study Commission; and

(16) Repealed by S.L. 2011-291, § 2.50, eff. June 24, 2011.

(17) The standing Committees on Pensions and Retirement.

(b) Reasonable public notice of all meetings of commissions, committees, and standing subcommittees of the General Assembly shall be given. For purposes of this subsection, "reasonable public notice" includes, but is not limited to:

(1) Notice given openly at a session of the Senate or of the House; or

(2) Notice mailed or sent by electronic mail to those who have requested notice, and to the Legislative Services Office, which shall post the notice on the General Assembly web site.

G.S. 143-318.12 shall not apply to meetings of commissions, committees, and standing subcommittees of the General Assembly.

(c) A commission, committee, or standing subcommittee of the General Assembly may take final action only in an open meeting.

(d) A violation of this section by members of the General Assembly shall be punishable as prescribed by the rules of the House or the Senate.

(e) The following sections shall apply to meetings of commissions, committees, and standing subcommittees of the General Assembly: G.S. 143-318.10(e) and G.S. 143-318.11,

G.S. 143-318.13 and G.S. 143-318.14, G.S. 143-318.16 through G.S. 143-318.17.

§ 143-318.15. Repealed by S.L. 2006-203, § 94, eff. July 1, 2007.

§ 143-318.16. Injunctive relief against violations of Article.

(a) The General Court of Justice has jurisdiction to enter mandatory or prohibitory injunctions to enjoin (i) threatened violations of this Article, (ii) the recurrence of past violations of this Article, or (iii) continuing violations of this Article. Any person may bring an action in the appropriate division of the General Court of Justice seeking such an injunction; and the plaintiff need not allege or prove special damage different from that suffered by the public at large. It is not a defense to such an action that there is an adequate remedy at law.

(b) Any injunction entered pursuant to this section shall describe the acts enjoined with reference to the violations of this Article that have been proved in the action.

(c) Repealed by Laws 1985 (Reg. Sess., 1986), c. 932, § 3, eff. Oct. 1, 1986.

§ 143-318.16A. Additional remedies for violations of Article.

(a) Any person may institute a suit in the superior court requesting the entry of a judgment declaring that any action of a public body was taken, considered, discussed, or deliberated in violation of this Article. Upon such a finding, the court may declare any such action null and void. Any person may seek such a declaratory judgment, and the plaintiff need not allege or prove special damage different from that suffered by the public at large. The public body whose action the suit seeks to set aside shall be made a party. The court may order other persons be made parties if they have or claim any right, title, or interest that would be directly affected by a declaratory judgment voiding the action that the suit seeks to set aside.

(b) A suit seeking declaratory relief under this section must be commenced within 45 days following the initial disclosure of the action that the suit seeks to have declared null and void; provided, however, that any suit for declaratory judgment brought pursuant to this section that seeks to set aside a bond order or bond referendum shall be commenced within the limitation periods prescribed by G.S. 159-59 and G.S. 159-62. If the challenged action is recorded in the minutes of the public body, its initial disclosure shall be deemed to have occurred on the date the minutes are first available for public inspection. If the challenged action is not recorded in the minutes of the public body, the date of its initial disclosure shall be determined by the court based on a finding as to when the plaintiff knew or should have known that the challenged action had been taken.

(c) In making the determination whether to declare the challenged action null and void, the court shall consider the following and any other relevant factors:

(1) The extent to which the violation affected the substance of the challenged action;

(2) The extent to which the violation thwarted or impaired access to meetings or proceedings that the public had a right to attend;

(3) The extent to which the violation prevented or impaired public knowledge or understanding of the people's business;

(4) Whether the violation was an isolated occurrence, or was a part of a continuing pattern of violations of this Article by the public body;

(5) The extent to which persons relied upon the validity of the challenged action, and the effect on such persons of declaring the challenged action void;

(6) Whether the violation was committed in bad faith for the purpose of evading or subverting the public policy embodied in this Article.

(d) A declaratory judgment pursuant to this section may be entered as an alternative to, or in combination with, an injunction entered pursuant to G.S. 143-318.16.

(e) The validity of any enacted law or joint resolution or passed simple resolution of either house of the General Assembly is not affected by this Article.

§ 143-318.16B. Assessments and awards of attorneys' fees.

When an action is brought pursuant to G.S. 143-318.16 or G.S. 143-318.16A, the court may make written findings specifying the prevailing party or parties, and may award the prevailing party or parties a reasonable attorney's fee, to be taxed against the losing party or parties as part of the costs. The court may order that all or any portion of any fee as assessed be paid personally by any individual member or members of the public body found by the court to have knowingly or intentionally committed the violation; provided, that no order against any individual member shall issue in any case where the public body or that individual member seeks the advice of an attorney, and such advice is followed.

§ 143-318.16C. Accelerated hearing; priority.

Actions brought pursuant to G.S. 143-318.16 or G.S. 143-318.16A shall be set down for immediate hearing, and subsequent proceedings in such actions shall be accorded priority by the trial and appellate courts.

§ 143-318.16D. Local acts.

Any reference in any city charter or local act to an "executive session" is amended to read "closed session".

§ 143-318.17. Disruptions of official meetings.

A person who willfully interrupts, disturbs, or disrupts an official meeting and who, upon being directed to leave the meeting by the presiding officer, willfully refuses to leave the meeting is guilty of a Class 2 misdemeanor.

§ 143-318.18. Exceptions.

This Article does not apply to:

(1) Grand and petit juries.

(2) Any public body that is specifically authorized or directed by law to meet in executive or confidential session, to the extent of the authorization or direction.

(3) The Judicial Standards Commission.

(3a) The North Carolina Innocence Inquiry Commission.

(4) Repealed by Laws 1991, c. 694, § 9.

(4a) The Legislative Ethics Committee.

(4b) A conference committee of the General Assembly.

(4c) A caucus by members of the General Assembly; however, no member of the General Assembly shall participate in a caucus which is called for the purpose of evading or subverting this Article.

(5) Law enforcement agencies.

(6) A public body authorized to investigate, examine, or determine the character and other qualifications of applicants for professional or occupational licenses or certificates or to take disciplinary actions against persons holding such licenses or certificates, (i) while preparing, approving, administering, or grading examinations or (ii) while meeting with respect to an individual applicant for or holder of such a license or certificate. This exception does not amend, repeal, or supersede any other statute that requires a public hearing or other practice and procedure in a proceeding before such a public body.

(7) Any public body subject to the State Budget Act, Chapter 143C of the General Statutes and exercising quasi-judicial functions, during a meeting or session

held solely for the purpose of making a decision in an adjudicatory action or proceeding.

(8)   The boards of trustees of endowment funds authorized by G.S. 116-36 or G.S. 116-238.

(9)   Repealed by Laws 1991, c. 694, § 9.

(10) Repealed by S.L. 2013-234, § 10, eff. July 3, 2013.

(11) The General Court of Justice.